Charley's Aunt

A PLAY IN THREE ACTS

by Brandon Thomas

This Acting Edition is printed from the MSS by Brandon
Thomas as first performed in 1892 and without the modernisations used in French's Acting Edition No. 470, first published
in 1935.

The copyright has now been assigned to Jevan Roderick
Brandon-Thomas, Amy Marguerite Brandon Barnes-Brand
and Silvia Brandon-Thomas.

SAMUEL FRENCH

25 West 45th St.   NEW YORK 19

7623 Sunset Blvd. HOLLYWOOD 46

LONDON   TORONTO

CHARLEY'S AUNT

Press and bindery of The Conway Printing Co.
New York

CHARLEY'S AUNT

STORY OF THE PLAY

This is the world-famous farce which has moved millions to tears of laughter. Jack Chesney, violently in love with Kitty Verdun, and Charles, equally enamoured of Miss Spettigue, invite the young ladies to their rooms for luncheon—in order to meet Charley's wealthy aunt from Brazil ("where the nuts come from"). But alas, the millionaire aunt sends word that she will have to defer her visit for a few days. What is to be done? The dear young things must not be compromised—no, never!—but neither will the youths give up the opportunity of declaring their love. The problem is solved by forcing another Oxford undergraduate into a black satin skirt, a lace fichu, a pair of mitts, an old-fashioned cap and wig. As Charley's Aunt then, this old frump is introduced to the sweethearts, to Jack's father (who is advised by the son to marry her millions), and to Stephen Spettigue, Miss Spettigue's guardian. The sweethearts hug and kiss Charley's dear old aunt; the two men make love to her. Then the real aunt turns up, assumes another name. In the comic confusion which results, young Lord Babberley, posing as the aunt, tricks Stephen Spettigue into agreeing to the marriage of his ward to Charley, the real aunt marries Jack's father, Jack gets Miss Verdun, and "Charley's Aunt" regains the fortune he lost at gambling and obtains the hand of the girl he loves. In its many stage and motion picture revivals, this play has never failed to reach a wide and eager audience.

3

NOTE.

As it is now an anomaly to stage "CHARLEY'S AUNT" in any other costume than the clothes of the original period of 1892, we have eliminated the slight modernisations we introduced in the first published edition, and now issue the original text exactly as written by BRANDON THOMAS and produced by him in 1892.

AMY BRANDON-THOMAS.

JEVAN BRANDON-THOMAS.

SILVIA BRANDON-THOMAS.

CHARLEY'S AUNT

Produced at the Royalty Theatre, London, on December 21st, 1892, transferred to the Globe Theatre. Original London Run, four years.

CAST

STEPHEN SPETTIGUE .... *Mr. Ernest Hendrie*
COLONEL SIR FRANCIS CHESNEY, BART
                      —*Mr. Brandon Thomas*
JACK CHESNEY .... *Mr. Percy Lyndal*
CHARLEY WYKEHAM .... *Mr. H. Farmer*
LORD FANCOURT BABBERLEY ...... *Mr. W. S. Penley*
BRASSETT .... *Mr. Cecil Thornbury*
DONNA LUCIA D' ALVADOREZ ...... *Miss Ada Branson*
AMY SPETTIGUE .... *Miss Kate Gordon*
KITTY VERDUN .... *Miss Nina Boucicault*
ELA DELAHAY .... *Miss Emily Cudmore*

Commemoration Week, Oxford, 1892

SYNOPSIS OF SCENES

ACT I

Jack Chesney's Rooms in College. (Morning).
"When pious frauds—are dispensations."—*Hudibras.*

ACT II

Garden outside Jack Chesney's Rooms. (Afternoon)
"While there's tea there's hope."—*Pinero.*

ACT III

Drawing Room at Spettigue's House. (Evening).
"Dinner lubricates business."—*Boswell.*

CHARLEY'S AUNT

Produced at the Standard Theatre, New York, October 2, 1894.

CAST

STEPHEN SPETTIGUE .... *W. J. Ferguson*
COL. SIR FRANCIS CHESNEY .... *Frank Burbeck*
JACK CHESNEY .... *Percy Lyndal*
CHARLEY WYKEHAM .... *Henry Woodruff*
LORD FANCOURT BABBERLEY ...... *Etienne Girardot*
BRASSETT .... *Henry Lillford*
THE NEW FOOTMAN .... *Charles Henderson*
DONNA LUCIA D' ALVADOREZ .... *Ellie Wilton*
KITTY VERDUN .... *Nanette Comstock*
AMY SFETTIGUE .... *Hattie Harvey*
ELA DELAHAY .... *Jessie Busley*

CHARLEY'S AUNT

CHARACTERS

COLONEL SIR FRANCIS CHESNEY, BART; *Late Indian Service*

STEPHEN SPETTIGUE; *Solicitor, Oxford*

JACK CHESNEY;

CHARLES WYKEHAM; } *Undergraduates at St. Olde's College, Oxford.*

LORD FANCOURT BABBERLEY;

BRASSETT; *A College Scout*

DONNA LUCIA D' ALVADOREZ; *From Brazil*

KITTY VERDUN; SPETTIGUE'S *Ward*

AMY SPETTIGUE; SPETTIGUE'S *Niece*

ELA DELAHAY; *An Orphan*

Charley's Aunt

ACT ONE

"When pious frauds—are dispensations."—Hudibras.

SCENE.—*Interior of Jack Chesney's Rooms, St. Olde's College, Oxford. Morning.*
   The walls are oak panelled or half-panelled or plain cream-washed walls with beautiful, low heraldic ceiling in cream, picked out in colour and dull gold. Door opening off, with passage backing, leading to outer door L.I.E. Door opening off to bedroom, with light backing, L.U.E. Between doors an oak sideboard with cupboard underneath. Large opening and recess with portiere to draw L.C. Long stone-mullioned embayed window R.C. with view of quad and practicable centre casement, to open off, window seat with four river cushions and one magazine. Long red rep fabric curtains. Upright piano C. with pile of music on top between window and recess. Fireplace R., looking-glass, etc., on mantel, low bookcases R. and L. of it. Saddle back armchair by fire with white antimacassar. Table C. with ashtray and books and table cover in dark material on it with two single chairs R. and L. of it, with sweater over back of L. chair. Writing-table down R.C. by fire, with A.B.C. time-table, magazine and "Corona" cigar-box. Stage cloth. Circular hat stand inside R.C. corner of recess with boxing gloves, single sticks, etc. on it. Plaster bust of Plato on pedestal L. corner of room—angle. Clock and photographs of chorus girls and flowers on mantelshelf, more photographs

*and books on top of book-cases, pipes, tobacco jars,
etc. Prints on walls above. Tray with three tumblers,
one square decanter half full of whiskey, one glass
jug of water on sideboard, four champagne bottles,
one bottle of claret (open) in sideboard cupboard.
Above on wall* L. *groups of Rowing Eights, foot-
ball teams. Six dining-room chairs arranged as
follows: two* R. *and* L. *of* C. *table, one below door*
L.I.E., *one at piano, one* L. *side of writing-table, one
top* R. *corner by window. Antique furniture, well-
worn comfortable chairs. Quad seen through window and sunlight streams in through window.*

CURTAIN MUSIC: *"The Eton Boating Song," by*
*A. D. E. W. Orchestra plays first 16 bars with grad-
ual crescendo—*CURTAIN *starts to rise—orchestra
plays next 16 bars more softly with gradual dimin-
uendo till music ceases at full rise of curtain.*

JACK *discovered seated at writing-table, unlit pipe
in mouth, struggling wildly to write a letter. He looks
at letter and tears it up.*

JACK CHESNEY: *Tall, dark, good-looking, about
twenty-two, wears light-coloured lounge suit and
college tie, leander pink and white diagonal stripes.
He laughs his way through life, is self-confident,
quick, alert and must have "drive"; as he sets the
pace of the play.*

JACK. I can't! I can't get into the vein. *(Flings down
pen.)* I don't know what to say—don't know how to
begin. I wish to goodness I'd spoken to her at the
dance the other evening, *(rises, to* C.*)* when she told me
they were all going away for the summer; instead, I've
gone and left everything till the last minute, and now
I'm regularly nonplussed. By George! I know what I'll
do. I'll make an exercise of it. I'll write it out a dozen
different ways, and send the one I think looks the

best. *(Goes back to table and sits, takes up pen.)* So come on, Jack, here we are, in love with the dearest girl on earth—tackle her like a man, and tell her so, or they'll be off north, you'll be gone down, and have lost your chance for ever. She's my fate, and I'm hanged if I shan't be hers! So here goes. *(Writing.)* "My Darling"! *(Stops.)* Rather strong, perhaps, to begin with. *(Tears up paper, places on* L. *of writing-table, begins again.)* "My Dear Miss Verdun—" *(Stops again.)* No, too formal—and not a bit what I really feel. *(Tears that up.)* "My Dear—" Hang it, why not? *(Writes boldly.)* "My Dear Kitty"! That's grand!

(BRASSETT *enters quietly door* L.U.E. *to table* C.)

(BRASSETT : *College Scout (manservant) between forty and fifty years of age, wears dark trousers and short dark grey alpaca coat, white collar and dark tie. He is always polite and never familiar in his manner.)*

Now I can go ahead like a house on fire. *(Looking proudly at letter.)* "My Dear Kitty, I—"

BRASSETT. I beg pardon, sir, but would you mind—?

JACK. Yes, very much; go away, I'm busy.

BRASSETT. Yes, sir, but—

JACK. I'm busy with the most important affair; get out!

BRASSETT *(raising book or two off table, and hesitating).* Yes, sir.

JACK *(aside).* Just as I'd made such a good start, too! *(At letter again.)* "My Dear Kitty—"

(BRASSETT *calmly drops books back on table.)*

(Aloud.) What are you doing, Brassett? Confound it all, what do you want?

BRASSETT. I merely wish to say, sir, that I have laid out a few things which—

JACK. All right, thank you, get out and leave me alone.

BRASSETT. Which I thought you wouldn't care to—

JACK *(in despair)*. Take 'em—keep 'em! Take every blessed rag I've got—only go away!

(BRASSETT *goes to door* L.U.E.)

(At letter again, savagely.) "My Dear Kitty—"

BRASSETT *(at door)*. Beg pardon, sir?

JACK. Confound it! I wasn't addressing *you*—go away!

(Exit BRASSETT, L.U.E., *quickly. Enter* CHARLEY, L.I. E., *with letter, comes* C. CHARLES WYKEHAM *is about twenty, good-looking, medium height, fair, Saxon type, charming and though shy is not awkward. Rowing type, wears white flannels, blazer and muffler, cheap watch in breast pocket of blazer with short chain hanging out. For later entrance with telegram —has changed blazer for a lounge suit coat, removed muffler and wears a collar and tie.)*

"My Dear Kitty—"

CHARLEY *(mildly)*. I say—! *(To* C.)

JACK. *(throwing down pen, jumping up savagely)*. If you don't clear out, Brassett, I'll— *(Meets* CHARLEY C.) Oh, it's you, Charley! What is it, old chap?

CHARLEY. Nothing, Jack. I don't want to interrupt you if you're busy. *(Going.)*

JACK *(going* C.) It's all right, Charley, don't go, it's only that fool Brassett.

CHARLEY. What's he doing? *(Coming back to* C.)

JACK. Only bagging all my clothes because I'm going down, and worrying me like Old Harry while I'm trying to write a-most-important-letter. *(Moving towards table* R.) Don't mind me to-day; I'm nervous and naggy and nonplussed. *(Sits on end of table* R.C.)

CHARLEY. And so am I, Jack.

JACK. Why?

CHARLEY. I've been trying to write a letter, too.

JACK. A letter! To whom?

CHARLEY. To—to Miss Spettigue.

JACK *(going to* CHARLEY, C.*)*. How far have *you* got?

(Both C.*)*

CHARLEY *(brightening)*. Oh! I began awfully well, but—I didn't want to be too distant, and I didn't like to be too—too—

JACK. Familiar? Well?

CHARLEY. So I just said, "My Dear Amy"—and then words failed me, and I've come to you for advice. You always know what to say and do.

JACK *(dubiously, with a look towards letter)*. Oh! Do I?

CHARLEY. You know my idiotic complaint; I'm shy —you're not.

JACK. Aren't I?

CHARLEY. So prescribe for me, old chap. What am I to say? *(Turning away* L., *sits* R. *corner of table* C.*)*

JACK *(going* R.C., *aside)*. A good idea! I'll prescribe for *him* and take the medicine myself. *(Sits at writing-table* R., *gets paper, etc. Energetically.)* Now then, let's see. You're in love with Amy Spettigue, and you want to know if there's any hope for you, and if so—

CHARLEY. You see, they're all off to Scotland to-morrow.

JACK. Yes, I know, and you want to see her at once. When and where?—bearer waits. Do I diagnose the case accurately?

CHARLEY. To a "Tee," old chap!

JACK. Very well then; you'll want to say something to this effect: *(writing)* "My Dear Kitty—" *(Stops dead.)*

CHARLEY *(going to him, writing-table* R.C.*)*. No—not Kitty—Amy.

JACK. Oh, of course. what am I thinking of? *(Tears up paper, takes fresh sheet. In casual, glib tone, writing.)* "My Dearest Amy— Forgive me, darling, for thus addressing you, but I love you so deeply"—underlined—

CHARLEY *(surprised, moving nearer—interrupting).* Rather strong, Jack.

JACK. Shut up! "So earnestly"—also underlined—

CHARLEY. Oh, I say! *(Turning away* c.)

JACK. "That I *must* write and tell you so. All I ask is—"

CHARLEY *(sits table* c.). But there's one obstacle to my putting it quite as straight as that, much as I'd *like* to.

JACK. What's that?

CHARLEY. Well—er—I've an *aunt.*

JACK. My dear Charley, most of us have; what about her?

CHARLEY. I feel I ought to tell her first.

JACK *(flings down pen, rises and goes to fireplace).* Oh! If you're going to drag an *aunt* into the business, we may as well wait till they all come back from Scotland.

CHARLEY. Why?

JACK. You know what "auntie" is when *she* steps in.

CHARLEY. No, I don't. That's just it; I *don't* know her. I've never even *seen* her.

JACK. Well, we won't be too hard on *that* aunt; she hasn't interfered much in your affairs up to now.

CHARLEY. Except to find out that I was an orphan and have me sent to Eton, and to Oxford; and now my guardian writes to me that she's coming here this morning by an early train, and will take luncheon with me at one o'clock.

JACK *(coming down to back of chair* L. *of writing table).* And you've never seen her?

CHARLEY. No. She went out to Brazil before I was

born, and became a sort of secretary to a very rich old
Brazilian chap out there, called Dom Pedro d'Alvadorez;
and now—by the merest accident in the world *(taking
"Truth" from pocket and pointing to marked paragraph)* I've seen this. *(Gives* JACK *paper.)*

JACK *(going down* R. NOTE: *"Lucia" is pronounced
"LOOSIA"—Portuguese, NOT Spanish. Reading.)*
"Madam—or rather Donna Lucia d'Alvadorez, the
Brazilian millionaire, who has taken Lord Toppleby's
magnificent mansion in Belgravia, is an English-woman
of genial disposition, and a financial genius. Indeed, it
was her capacity in this direction that earned the grati-
tude of her late husband, and led to a romantic death-
bed marriage." *(To* CHARLEY.) Well, I don't see much
in that! *(Offering paper back.)*

CHARLEY. Go on, Jack, read the next.

JACK *(reading)*. "Her only relation—is a nephew at
Oxford"—lucky nephew!

CHARLEY. That's me.

JACK. By George, Charley, this is a startler! *(Throws
paper to* CHARLEY.) And she may be here any minute?
(Goes to mantelpiece, looks at clock.)

CHARLEY. I've met all the trains up to now. I wish
she'd have come some other day. *(Rises, moves away
down* L. *a little.)*

JACK *(turning, looks at clock)*. She'll arrive by the
next, just in time for lunch.

CHARLEY *(dolefully)*. Yes, it's a bore. I wanted to
write that letter to Amy.

JACK *(sits on table* R.C., *thinking)*. I don't know so
much about that!

CHARLEY *(comes* C.). But it's an awfully difficult
letter to write—fearfully complicated.

JACK. Why?

CHARLEY. Well, you see, I've no people or anything.

JACK. "No people," with an aunt like that! *(Pointing
to paper which is in* CHARLEY's *hand.)*

CHARLEY. But I've no reason to expect anything
from her—more than she's already done for me—for

which, of course, I'm very grateful and all that—but I want to see Amy and put it to her that if—

JACK (*suddenly—coming* C. *to* CHARLEY). Charley! I've got a clinking good idea!

CHARLEY (*pushing* JACK *towards writing-table—gratefully*). Jack, you are a good chap! Write it down and I'll copy it out.

JACK (*stopping him*). No, not for you—for me—for us both. You're gone on Amy—I'm in love with Kitty.

CHARLEY. Really, Jack?

JACK. Madly. Worse than anything I ever took up—even cricket! I was writing to tell her so when you came in. (*Pointing.*) There's the letter.

CHARLEY (*wringing* JACK'S *hand with effusion*). I'm so glad! and what's your "idea"?

JACK. Hang letter-writing! We'll give a luncheon party for your aunt, tea afterwards in the garden.

CHARLEY. In the garden?

JACK. Yes, I'll get leave.

CHARLEY. But my rooms are so small.

JACK. Never mind, I'll lend you mine. (*Pushing* CHARLEY *towards writing-table chair* C.) Brassett shall see to it. (*Calling towards* L.) Brassett! (*To* CHARLEY.) Now, come on! First we'll ask the girls.

CHARLEY. Ask the girls? (*Standing behind writing-table.*)

JACK (*by chair* L. *of writing-table*). To meet your aunt.

CHARLEY. What about old Spettigue?

JACK. Blow old Spettigue!

CHARLEY. Oh, I forgot. He's up in town for a few days on business. (*Sits at writing-table.*)

JACK. So much the better. (*Calling.*) Brassett!

CHARLEY. Do you think they'll come?

JACK. They'll jump at it.

CHARLEY. What makes you think so?

JACK. Well, what do you think?

CHARLEY. Why, Jack, you know, I rather agree with you.

JACK. We'll send a note at once—you write it—go ahead.

(CHARLEY writes to dictation.)

"My Dear Miss Spettigue—" *(Calling.)* Brassett, where are you?

(BRASSETT, L.U.E., and comes down L. of JACK.)

Where *are* you? *(Turns, sees BRASSETT standing L.)* Oh—er, Brassett, get someone to take a note to Mr. Spettigue's.

BRASSETT. Yes, sir.

(Exits L.I.E.)

CHARLEY. Yes, Jack, I've got that.

JACK *(gets envelope, pen and book to write on)*. "Would you and Miss Verdun—" *(puts foot on chair L. of writing-table and puts cigar-box on knee to write on)* "do me the honour—"

CHARLEY *(repeating)*. —"the honour"—

JACK. —"to lunch with me and Mr. Chesney:"

CHARLEY *(repeating.)* —"Mr. Chesney"—

JACK. I'll address the envelope.

CHARLEY *(still repeating—while dipping pen in ink)*. "I'll address the—"

JACK *(breaking in before CHARLEY can write it)*. No, not that, you muff! "At his room, St. Olde's College, to-day at one o'clock." *(Addressing envelope.)* Miss Spettigue—

CHARLEY. Miss— *(about to write)*.

(JACK stops him before he writes.)

JACK. No, look out! "To meet my aunt—" What did you say her name was, Charley?

CHARLEY. Donna Lucia d'Alvadorez.

JACK. "Donna"— All right, stick it down. "An answer by bearer will greatly oblige." *(Blots envelope.)*

CHARLEY *(writing)*. "Yours sincerely. Charles Wykeham. *(Blots and folds letter.)* Splendid, Jack, you're a genius! *(Hands letter to JACK.)*

JACK *(takes letter, puts it in envelope and closes it)*. It's a glorious opportunity. They're off to Scotland.

CHARLEY. And we're off "down."

JACK. And now we shall have them all to ourselves. *(Going L.C.)*

(Re-enter BRASSETT, L.I.E.)

BRASSETT. The messenger, sir.

JACK *(gives letter to BRASSETT)*. Give him that, and tell him to look sharp. *(Turns back slowly to CHARLEY.)*

BRASSETT. Yes, sir.

(Going L. At door quick glance at address on envelope, smiles and exits L.I.E.)

JACK *(returning to table, takes up torn letters)*. This sort of thing is not to be settled by correspondence. *(Tears up letters, gives fragments to CHARLEY, who puts them into paper basket.)*

CHARLEY. No, and we shall have them all to ourselves.

JACK. Yes, and we couldn't have asked them if it hadn't been for your aunt. I'm beginning to love that dear old lady already. *(Calling.)* Brassett!

(Re-enter BRASSETT, L.I.E.)

BRASSETT. Yes, sir?

JACK. Lunch for five.

BRASSETT. For how many, sir?

JACK. For five. *(Going to him.)*

BRASSETT. For five, sir? *(Laughs quietly.)*

(CHARLEY *rises and goes over to them.*)

JACK (*to* BRASSETT). What are you laughing at?

BRASSETT. Well, sir, I'm afraid our credit in the kitchen is somewhat exhausted. (*Pronounced "hegs-austed" by taking a catch-breath in the middle.*)

JACK (*to* BRASSETT). Oh, is it? (*Turning to* CHARLEY.) How are you off for "tick," Charley?

CHARLEY. Well, Jack, I'm afraid my guardian's rather—er—

JACK. Oh, is he? (*Pause, then to* BRASSETT.) Never mind, Brassett, get it outside—go to Bunter's.

BRASSETT (*shaking head doubtfully*). I'm afraid, sir, we owe Bunter's—

JACK. Oh, do we? (*Turns to* CHARLEY *and sees his watch-chain.*) Charley, you don't mind (*takes watch and chain off* CHARLEY) it'll be all right when my cheque comes? (*Gives them to* BRASSETT.) Here you are, Brassett, do the best you can with that.

BRASSETT (*taking them and looking at watch critically*). This is no good, sir. I couldn't get anything on this, sir. (*Hands it back to* JACK.) However, sir I've no doubt it will be all right at Bunter's, if I say it's for *me.* (*Goes behind table* C.)

(CHARLEY *goes to chair* L. *of writing-table and sits.*)

JACK (*laughing*). Oh, all right, Brassett; lunch for *five* at one o'clock. (*Goes down* L.)

BRASSETT (*looks at own gold watch*). Rather short notice, sir. (*Takes books off table* C. *and puts them on sideboard* L.)

JACK. All right, long pay; go where you like, do what you like, only lunch for *five* at one. (*Putting watch and chain in his own waistcoat pocket, crossing to* CHARLEY.) That's all right, Charley, isn't it?

CHARLEY (*to* JACK). I say, Jack, (*taking watch and chain*) that's *my* watch!

JACK. I beg your pardon, old chap, my mistake.

BRASSETT (*at sideboard*). What wine, sir?

JACK. Champagne.

BRASSETT (*sulkily*). Very little left, sir. (*Opens sideboard.*)

JACK. Half a dozen bottles! (R. *of* C. *table.*)

BRASSETT (*imperturably*). No, sir, I think not; (*getting out four from sideboard cupboard*) only four, sir. (*Puts them on sideboard.*)

CHARLEY. Oh, quite enough.

JACK (*to* BRASSETT, *aggressively*). Six, I'll swear.

BRASSETT. Pardon me, sir—only four of champagne— (*puts them on table* C.) and I think (*taking out bottle of opened claret*) yes, one of claret. (*Holding it up.*)

JACK. Oh, hang that claret!

(BRASSETT *puts it on sideboard.*)

It's been open a month. All right. (*Aside to* CHARLEY). He's sneaked those other two bottles. He's a corker!

(BRASSETT *comes down* L.C.)

CHARLEY. My fellow's just the same.

(JACK *gives ferocious glance at* BRASSETT, *who returns it imperturbably.*)

JACK. They all are!

(BRASSETT *exits* L.I.E.)

Now, while you and your dear old aunt are looking at the chapel and the cloisters, Kitty and I can have our little talk.

CHARLEY. Yes, Jack, that's all very well, but what about Amy and me, and our little talk? She'll be in our way horribly.

JACK. I never thought of that.

CHARLEY. She's all very well as an excuse to get the girls to come here—but by herself she'll be an awful bore.

JACK. She'll be worse than that. She'll be a brute of a nuisance. *(Sits on table C.)*

CHARLEY. What shall we do?

JACK. Well, Napoleon went over the Alps on horseback, and I've been under them by train, so there must be a way out of this.

CHARLEY. But how? Couldn't we ask someone to meet her?

JACK. Yes. Someone we can depend upon.

(Re-enter BRASSETT, L.I.E. Busies himself at sideboard.)

CHARLEY. But whom?

JACK *(sees BRASSETT; aside to CHARLEY)*. What about Brassett? He's a pompous sort of chap, and as artful as a corkscrew, can't we turn him into a Don, or something, for the day?

CHARLEY *(dubiously)*. Yes, that's a good idea, Jack, but—

JACK *(after another look at BRASSETT)*. No, won't do—we shall want him to wait at table.

CHARLEY. Oh, of course, so we shall.

JACK. There's Freddy Peel.

CHARLEY. Oh, he's such a cynical chap.

(BRASSETT exits through recess up L.)

JACK *(sits again on table C.)*. Besides, he'd neglect your aunt.

CHARLEY. Yes, and want to make love to our girls.

JACK *(suddenly)*. By George, I've got it! *Babbs— Fanny Babbs!* We'll ask *him.*

CHARLEY. Oh yes; why didn't we think of him before?

JACK. He's a jolly cheerful little chap. Will amuse your aunt like the deuce and keep her in a rattling good humour.

CHARLEY *(comes to* JACK). Splendid'

JACK. Brassett!

(BRASSETT *re-enters, comes down* L.C.)

BRASSETT. Yes, sir.

JACK. Go to Lord Fancourt Babberley's rooms, give him my compliments and ask him to come here at once.

BRASSETT. Yes, sir. *(Goes to door* L.I.E.)

CHARLEY *(crossing* L. *to* BRASSETT). Say it's very important.

BRASSETT *(as he goes)*. Yes, sir.

(Exits L.I.E.)

JACK *(shouting after* BRASSETT). And very immed· iate!

BRASSETT *(speaks off)*. Yes, sir.

JACK *(crossing to fireplace)*. And while Babbs is doing "gooseberry" with your aunt, we can have our chat with the girls.

CHARLEY *(sits on table* C.). By the by, Jack, talking of Babbs' cheerfulness, haven't you noticed something about him lately—ever since he was so ill and had to go off to the Mediterranean?

JACK. I've noticed he's been jolly hard up. *(Sits in chair back of writing-table.)*

CHARLEY. I fancy, from a few hints he's dropped to me, that he's a bit hard hit himself.

JACK. What, Babbs in love!

CHARLEY. Yes; and if I'm not much mistaken, he's as softhearted over a girl as—

JACK. We are. All the better! he'll feel for us. He'll see the necessity then of keeping the old lady well out of the way.

CHARLEY. By George, Jack, you'll be Prime Minister one of these days.

(Re-enter BRASSETT, *L.I.E.)*

BRASSETT. His lordship's compliments, sir, and he says he can't come, he has a luncheon party, and could you lend him a few bottles of champagne?

JACK *(rising)*. Lend him a few bottles of champagne! Well, of all the cheek!

CHARLEY *(seated on* C. *table)*. Who's he got coming?

JACK (R.C., *angrily)*. Oh, Freddy Peel, and a lot of idiots like himself, I expect, and they'll be howling comic songs all the afternoon.

CHARLEY. Yes, it'll sound awfully bad, won't it?

JACK. He mustn't! *(Crossing* L.C. *to* BRASSETT.) Here, Brassett, lay for six. *(Comes to* CHARLEY.)

BRASSETT. Yes, sir. *(Gets to back of table* C., *moves books to piano at back.)*

CHARLEY. What shall we do? *(Going to* JACK.)

JACK *(at door* L.I.E., *taking* CHARLEY *with him)*. Come on, we'll go to him, we must *make* him come, he can't upset all our plans in this selfish way. *(Puts* CHARLEY *across to* L.I.E. *To* BRASSETT.) Put that champagne in ice, Brassett. And tidy up my room. Come on, Charley, come on!

(Exeunt CHARLEY, *propelled by* JACK, *L.I.E.)*

BRASSETT *(annoyed)*. One o'clock! *(Looks helplessly at watch.)* Put room in order first—always the way! *(Opens windows wider, picks up book from window seat.)* Hurry, scurry, no time for anything. They come with a bang, they go with a bang, everything with a bang, except pay their bills with a bang. *(At door* L.U. E., *looking at champagne ruefully.)* Well, I did think that little perquisite was safe, 'pon my word I did!

(Exits L.U.E.)

LORD FANCOURT (*calling off* R.) Jack! I say, Jack old man.

(LORD FANCOURT BABBERLEY: *He is small, about five foot three to five foot six at most. Good-looking, humorous face, smartly dressed in light grey pepper-corn suit with waistcoat and black elastic-sided boots.*

He only removes his coat when he gets into the "Aunt's" dress. The suit must be light to show up well against the black petticoat and its elastic braces.

The essential thing to bear in mind when he is impersonating "The Aunt" is that LORD FANCOURT *has "never acted in his life before" or worn woman's clothes. He still walks, talks and moves like a man, and never attempts to "act the woman." No effemin-ate female impersonation business. He tries to lighten his voice when he is first introduced, and it cracks appallingly. After that he speaks naturally, but be-ing careful not to use the deep tones of his voice except to* JACK, CHARLEY *and* BRASSETT, *who know who he really is, or again when he forgets he is sup·· posed to be a woman. He just looks a nice old lady of the Victorian era.*)

(LORD FANCOURT BABBERLEY *appears at window up* R. c., *carrying a large Gladstone bag.*)

LORD FANCOURT (*climbing in at window*). Where the Dickens are you? (*Looks hurriedly in bedroom* L. U.E.) I wanted to borrow some fizz. (*Goes to cabinet* L.) I wonder where they keep it. (*Turns and sees champagne on* C. *table.*) Hallo! By George—the very thing! (*Puts bag on table and opens it. Starts wrapping up first bottle with antimacassar from chair* R.C.) Serves him right, he shouldn't leave it about (*puts first bottle in bag*) in this ostentatious way (*puts second bottle in bag, wrapping third bottle with another antimacassar or scarf from chair* L.C.) when I'm so beastly hard up. (*Puts third bottle in bag.*) Won't they be jolly waxy?

(Puts fourth bottle in bag and closing bag.) That's a bottle apiece *(comes* C. *with bag)* and they must make out with whiskey and soda. *(Going* L.)

(Enter JACK *and* CHARLEY, L.I.E. *They meet* LORD FANCOURT *at door and bring him back to* C., CHARLEY L. *of him,* JACK R. *of him.)*

JACK. Hallo, Babbs. *(Takes bag from* LORD FANCOURT, *puts it on table* C.) We've just been over to your rooms to find you. We've been talking about you.

LORD FANCOURT (C.). No, really? *(To* JACK.) I say, how do you think I'm looking?

JACK (R., *cheerily).* Splendid, old chap!

(CHARLEY L.)

LORD FANCOURT. Yes, I thought you'd be pleased with me. *(Takes bag and bolts towards* L.I.E.) Well, ta-ta!

(CHARLEY *stops him at door* L.I.E. *They bring him back as before.* JACK *takes bag from* LORD FANCOURT *and puts it on table* C.)

JACK. Don't go, Babbs; you wanted to see us, didn't you?

(All three down C. *as before.)*

LORD FANCOURT. Oh yes! I wanted to borrow some fizz, but—

JACK. Sorry I can't. I could have spared you a couple of bottles, but that fool Brassett—

LORD FANCOURT. I know. My fellow's just the same. There's no reasoning with them, is there? Well, ta-ta! *(Makes a feint to bolt.)*

(JACK *and* CHARLEY *miss him and land on* C. *table over bag.* LORD FANCOURT *grins.)*

JACK *(comes down* R., *to* LORD FANCOURT, C.). I looked you up last night, Babbs, but you were out.

(CHARLEY *comes down* L.)

LORD FANCOURT (C.). Yes. You know Freddy Peel, don't you? He's an awful idiot—hasn't a particle of brains, has he? But *I'm* all right! He gave a card party last night, and I won a hundred pounds from him. You should have seen his face! It makes me laugh now.

JACK. Why, Freddy Peel hasn't sixpence!

LORD FANCOURT. No, really?

CHARLEY. Did he pay you?

LORD FANCOURT. No, but he's going to—when his grandmother dies.

JACK. Why, the old lady's been dead years!

LORD FANCOURT. No, really? That's beastly! You know, I'm stumped, and he's had an awful lot out of me. But he's an awful idiot, hasn't a particle of brains, has he? But I'm all right! *(Picks up bag)* Ta-ta; I'm off! *(Attempts to bolt towards window.)*

(JACK *intercepts and brings him back to table as before.* JACK *puts bag on table.)*

JACK *(down* R.). I say, Babbs, we want you to stay and lunch with us to-day.

LORD FANCOUURT (C.). I say, you chaps, don't play the giddy goat! I've got to meet my tutor.

JACK *(with mock concern).* Babbs, you mustn't work like this. You're looking quite pulled down.

LORD FANCOUKT *(to* JACK). Am I really? *(Turns to* CHARLEY.)

CHARLEY. I was only telling Jack so just now.

LORD FANCOURT. Do you think I shall die? *(Turns to* JACK.)

JACK. Not you! You don't want to worry over all

this study. You'll be a great man of one sort or the other one of these days without all that.

LORD FANCOURT. Well, that's what *I* think, you know. But I ought to do something. We've had a wonderful lot of Johnnies in our family—great Johnnies in the army and navy and things!

JACK. I'll bet they never killed themselves with study!

LORD FANCOURT. No, but I must do *something*.

JACK. Of course, Babbs, you must stay to lunch. Charley's aunt is going to pay him a visit.

LORD FANCOURT. No, really? What fun! I know Charley visits his "uncle" sometimes, when he's hard up, *(pulling* CHARLEY'S *watch out by the chain)* so it's only right his aunt should return the visit.

(All laugh, pushing LORD FANCOURT *to and fro.* CHARLEY *regains his watch.)*

JACK. Now that's just the sort of thing we want— a jolly smart chap like you, with a fund of humour and a lot of brilliant coversation. *(Turns* LORD FANCOURT *round so that they face each other.)*

CHARLEY. Yes, Babbs, that's it! *(Hands on* LORD FANCOURT'S *shoulders and turns him round same as* JACK *has done, so that they face each other.)*

JACK *(pulls him back facing* C.*)*. To interest and amuse a charming lady.

LORD FANCOURT. Yes. Who is she?

JACK. Why, Charley's Aunt.

LORD FANCOURT. What's she like?

CHARLEY. Well, you see, Babbs, we don't quite know. I'm to see her to-day for the first time.

LORD FANCOURT. I say, Charley, she may turn out to be an awful old "croc."*

JACK. She's a widow, and a millionaire, that's enough, isn't it?

---

*"Croc," short for "crocodile." This was a slang expression of 1892; the modern equivalent would be "frump."

LORD FANCOURT. Rather! *(To* CHARLEY.) Put me down for a chance, Charley. I'll take a chance!

JACK. We didn't care to ask Freddy Peel, did we, Charley?

CHARLEY. No. *(Turning away* L.)

JACK. No.

LORD FANCOURT. No. He's an awful idiot!— I say, what's her name?

CHARLEY *(deliberately).* Donna Lucia d'Alvadorez.

LORD FANCOURT. Oh, dem it, what a name! *(Seizes bag again and bolts to door* L.)

(JACK *and* CHARLEY *bring him back,* R.C., *turn him round and run him up to table* C. *on which he falls face downwards, putting bag on table.* JACK *brings him down* C. *again.)*

JACK. Look here, Babbs, it's no use; you must stay to lunch. You'll find Charley's Aunt a *charming* old lady.

LORD FANCOURT. Charming *old* lady! I say, look here, haven't you got anything younger coming?

CHARLEY. Oh yes, two other ladies.

LORD FANCOURT. Nice? Young?

CHARLEY. Yes.

LORD FANCOURT. Ah! That's more in my line. How many did you say?

JACK. Two.

LORD FANCOURT. Oh, I see. One for each of you, and the old "croc" for me. No thanks, I'm off!

(LORD FANCOURT *bolts up* R. *of table* C. *towards window with his bag and is brought back as before.)*

JACK *(coming down* R. *of him).* Now listen, Babbs. This is an awfully serious affair.

LORD FANCOUURT (C.). I should think so, with an old "croc" like that!

CHARLEY *(coming down* L. *of him)*. And we want your *help* as a friend.

JACK. Yes, Babbs, a friend we can *trust,* eh?

LORD FANCOURT. Rather!

JACK. We'll take you into our confidence. No humbug —straight as a die. We're in love.

LORD FANCOURT. What, Charley as well? You silly ass! *(Pushes him away, sits on table* C.)

(CHARLEY *goes down* L.)

JACK. No fool of a flirtation business, but the real downright serious thing. *(Sits on corner of writing-table.)*

CHARLEY. And Babbs, if you knew the girls as well as we do, you wouldn't wonder at it.

JACK. And they're coming here to lunch to-day.

LORD FANCOURT. I say, have you proposed? *(From one to the other.)*

JACK. No, that's just it.

LORD FANCOURT. Oh, I see. You want me to propose for you?

JACK. *No!* We'll do that for ourselves. That's why we've asked them to come.

CHARLEY. You know, Babbs, you don't understand our feelings a bit.

LORD FANCOURT. Oh, don't I, though. I say— *(Rises, comes down* C., *beckons boys to him. All* C.) Haven't you noticed how sad I've been lately?

CHARLEY. Yes.

JACK. What is it?

LORD FANCOURT. Well, I don't know, but I think— I'm in love too.

CHARLEY. What makes you think that?

LORD FANCOURT. I'm always wanting to be alone, and hear the birds sing.

(JACK *and* CHARLEY *laugh.)*

And I'm getting so fond of poetry. I can't sleep. I took
to drink for a couple of days, but it made me ill for a
week, so I left it off.

JACK. You've got all the symptoms. Sit down and
tell us all about it.

(LORD FANCOURT *goes to chair* R. *of table* C. CHARLEY
sits on table C. JACK *sits at table* R. LORD FANCOURT
places his hat on CHARLEY'S *foot.* CHARLEY *removes
it.*)

LORD FANCOURT. You remember when I was
ploughed?

JACK. Beastly shame!

LORD FANCOURT. No, not last time—the term before. I was awfully ill, and took the yacht round to the
Mediterranean, and at Monte Carlo I came across an
English officer named Delahay—quite penniless and
dying. You know, Jack, he tried to commit suicide.

JACK. Bad luck at the tables, eh?

LORD FANCOURT. Yes. He'd beggared himself and
his only child, the sweetest little girl you ever saw,
Jack. And to amuse him and keep his spirits up, I
used to play cards with him.

CHARLEY. And what became of him?

LORD FANCOURT. He died, poor fellow!

JACK. And what became of her—the sweetest little
girl you ever saw?

LORD FANCOURT. I lost sight of her. A lady travel-
ling home that way—from South America, I believe—
took charge of her and brought her to England. You
know, Jack, I tried to tell her that—

JACK. You loved her?

LORD FANCOURT. But she was in such grief that—

JACK. It all oozed out of your finger-tips and the
points of your hair!

LORD FANCOURT. But after all, you know, I might
have been rejected and I should have looked a silly
ass.

JACK. At any rate, you can sympathise with us.

(Knock off L.I.E.*)*

(Enter BRASSETT L.U.E. *and exits* L.I.E.*)*

JACK. Hallo! Here's the messenger back.

*(*JACK, LORD FANCOURT *and* CHARLEY *all hurry across* L. BRASSETT *re-enters with note, hands it to* JACK *and goes up* L.C. *to sideboard, quietly arranges three tumblers, whiskey decanter and jug of water on tray during next scene.)*

(Opens letter and reads.) They're coming!

(They are looking over each other's shoulders while JACK *opens note.* LORD FANCOURT *takes note from* JACK.*)*

LORD FANCOURT. By Jove!

*(*CHARLEY *takes it from him.* LORD FANCOURT *is left staring at his thumb and two first fingers spread out.)*

CHARLEY. So they are! *(Goes* R. *and sits in writing-chair with his back to* JACK *and* LORD FANCOURT, *reading letter.)*
JACK. You'll stop, Babbs?
LORD FANCOURT. Oh, I say—look here— *(Looks at clothes.)*
JACK. No, you'll do as you are. We won't let you go now we've got you.
LORD FANCOURT. But look here, Jack, don't play the giddy goat; I've something else to do.
JACK. What is it?
LORD FANCOURT. It's something awfully important.
JACK. Well, what?

LORD FANCOURT. I'm going to play in some amateur theatricals.

JACK. Rot! He'll be ploughed again—won't he, Charley?

LORD FANCOURT. But I've given my word.

JACK. What are you playing?

LORD FANCOURT. A lady—an old lady—and I've never acted in my life before—

JACK. Oh! That's his tutor, eh, Charley?

LORD FANCOURT. And I'm going to try on the things before those fellows come.

JACK. You can try them on here. Where are they?

LORD FANCOURT. In my rooms, in a box on the bed, but—

(BRASSETT *at sideboard.*)

JACK *(to* BRASSETT). Fetch them, Brassett, quick!

(BRASSETT *exits* L.I.E. CHARLEY *goes up to window.*)

LORD FANCOURT. No, I'll fetch them with my little bag. *(Bolts* L.I.E. *with bag.)*

(JACK *intercepts him; they struggle for bag.* JACK *gets it and throws it casually down on table* C. LORD FANCOURT *picks it up very concerned, takes a step or two down and shakes bag gently to hear if any bottles are broken, then runs hand underneath to see if any are leaking—reassured, puts bag on chair* L. *of* C. *table. Neither* JACK *nor* CHARLEY *sees any of* LORD FANCOURT'S *business with bag.* JACK, *during this, gets whiskey, water and glasses on salver from sideboard, places them on* C. *table.* CHARLEY *coming down* R. *to* C. *table.* JACK *behind* C. *table.* LORD FANCOURT L. *of table.* JACK *pours out two whiskies, hands decanter to* CHARLEY.)

CHARLEY *(pouring out whiskey for himself, leaving*

decanter on R. *corner of table).* Babbs, **you don't** sympathise with us a bit!

(JACK *pours water into one whiskey.)*

LORD FANCOURT. Don't I though? I only wish I could see my own little girl!

JACK *(adding water to second whiskey).* Oh, she'll turn up one of these days. *(Offers drink to* LORD FANCOURT.) Have a drink?

(CHARLEY *adds water to his own whiskey.)*

LORD FANCOURT. No, I've knocked it off.

JACK. Just a small one.

LORD FANCOURT. I'm teetotal.

JACK. Oh, very well. Here you are, Charley. *(Offers glass to* CHARLEY.)

LORD FANCOURT. All right, I'll have it. *(Seizes glass.)*

JACK. I tell you what we'll do. We'll drink her health —wherever she is. Here's to the future Lady Fancourt Babberley. What did you say her name was?

LORD FANCOURT. Haven't the slightest idea!

(JACK *and* CHARLEY *laugh.)*

JACK. Go on with you! *(Lifts his glass.)* Miss Delahay.

(They drink. LORD FANCOURT *places his glass on table. Re-enter* BRASSETT *with dress-box,* L.I.E.—*a large brown cardboard box with gilt edges, like an exaggerated chocolate box.)*

BRASSETT. Your things, m'lord.

(CHARLEY *goes down* R., *sits chair side of writing-table.* JACK *goes* R.C. *front of* C. *table.)*

LORD FANCOURT *(taking box from* BRASSETT*)*
Thank you, Brassett. You're an awfully good chap.
(Crosses to JACK*; aside.)* I say, Jack, could you lend
me half a crown? *(Turns up-stage and puts box on
window seat at back.)*

(BRASSETT *at sideboard.)*

JACK *(feels in pockets, then aside to* CHARLEY*).*
Charley! Have you half-a-crown?

CHARLEY *(pulling out linings of trouser pockets).*
No, Jack, I haven't.

JACK *(crossing* L., *aside to* BRASSETT*).* Brassett!
Give me half-a-crown, will you?

BRASSETT. Yes, sir. *(Takes out handful of money—
gives half-a-crown.)*

JACK *(comes* C.*).* Babbs!

(LORD FANCOURT *comes down* R.C.)

(Aside to LORD FANCOURT.*)* Here you are. *(Gives half-
crown and crosses to* CHARLEY R.*)*

LORD FANCOURT. Thanks. *(Crosses to* BRASSETT,
L.*)* Brassett, here you are.

(JACK *and* CHARLEY *see half-crown given back to*
BRASSETT *and laugh.* CHARLEY *collapsed in chair*
L. *of writing-table.* JACK *ditto into chair* R. *of table*
C. LORD FANCOURT *turns, puzzled, crosses to* JACK.
JACK *whispers to him, points to* BRASSETT, *then
twice to himself, then to* LORD FANCOURT *and then
to* BRASSETT *again.* LORD FANCOURT *joins in laughter
and goes up to window seat and picks up dress-box.*
BRASSETT, *during this, removes bag from chair* L.
of table C. *to chair at back, and exits* L.U.E.*)*

JACK *(to* LORD FANCOURT, *pointing to box).* What
have you got there?

LORD FANCOURT. Chocolates.

CHARLEY. Chocolates? *(Still seated in chair.)*

JACK. Let's have a look!

LORD FANCOURT. No, I'll tell you what I'll do. I'll try them on after lunch while you're all in the garden.

JACK. You can't do that; we shall want you with us. Try them on now, won't take long, will it?

LORD FANCOURT. Only a minute or two. *(Lifts box on to his L. shoulder, crossing up-stage to L.)* I've lost an awful lot of time over these theatricals. *(At door.)* But next term I mean to work.

(Exits L.U.E. JACK goes up to front of fireplace.)

KITTY *(off)*. Oh yes, here it is, here's the name!

AMY *(off)*. Oh, so it is! "Mr. Chesney." I wonder if they're in.

(Knock.)

JACK *(to CHARLEY at chair)*. Here they are, and your aunt's not come yet. *(Rushes to mantelpiece to see the time, notices photographs, slams them face down, arranges tie, smoothes hair all in a hurry, returns below table C.)*

CHARLEY *(rises, getting behind JACK)*. Good gracious! What shall we do? *(Also trying to see in mirror.)*

(Re-enter BRASSETT, L.U.E., goes to door L.I.E.)

JACK. Oh, let them come in. We can explain. *(Crossing L.C. below table C.)* Show them in, Brassett.

(BRASSETT opens door, showing in KITTY and AMY, closes door and goes up back C., and then exits L.U.E.)

(Shaking hands with KITTY.) How do you do?

(Shaking hands with AMY.*)* So kind of you to come!
KITTY. Oh, we were very pleased to be able to come.

(They both cross to table R. CHARLEY *joins* AMY L.*)*

Weren't we, Amy?
AMY. Oh, yes. *(To* CHARLEY.*)* Mr. Wykeham, are
we too early?
CHARLEY. Oh no, no!

(They shake hands and move up to C. *table together.*
CHARLEY, *in his nervousness, backs into the chair,
then offers it to* AMY; *she sits chair* L. *of* C. *table.)*

KITTY. Yes, Mr. Chesney, you didn't mention any
time.

*(*JACK *gives chair,* KITTY *sits* L. *of writing-table.)*

JACK. Oh, not at all, not at all! We're delighted!
(Going to fireplace to look at clock. Aside.) She'll be
here soon.

(Enter LORD FANCOURT L.U.E., *in his shirt-sleeves—to*
C. *upstage, sees girls and bolts back* L.U.E. JACK *and*
CHARLEY *in terror the girls may see him.* CHARLEY,
*from behind table, leans over table, hides the drink,
etc., with his hat, on table* C. BRASSETT *takes tray
from table* C. *and off through recess up* L.C., *leaving whiskey decanter.* CHARLEY *leans forward talking to* AMY *and screening whiskey with his hat, at
the same time signalling with his hand behind his
back, to* JACK.*)*

KITTY *(sitting).* And this is where you think and
study and do all your work and everything?

*(*JACK *rapidly takes decanter from table* C., *hides it in
fireplace and returns to chair behind writing-table.)*

JACK. Oh yes, we do a lot of that sort of thing here. *(Sits.)*

KITTY. You've jolly quarters here.

(JACK and KITTY continue to talk aside.)

CHARLEY *(to AMY)*. I'm so glad you were able to come here to-day. You're off to Scotland to-morrow, and we shall miss you so much.

AMY. Yes, Uncle always takes us to some dreadfully remote place at this time of the year, where we never see a soul, and it's *so* dreary

CHARLEY. Why does he?

AMY. I don't know.

CHARLEY. It's a shame!

AMY. Why, are you sorry we're going?

CHARLEY. Sorry? Why, it's put me—and Jack—into a perfect fever; that's why we were so anxious to see you here to-day.

AMY. It's lucky uncle is away in town, or I don't think we could have come.

CHARLEY. Why?

AMY. I don't know, but he raises such odd objections, and then you know he's so peculiar about Kitty.

CHARLEY. Why?

AMY. She's an heiress, you know, and he's her guardian.

(They talk aside.)

JACK *(ardently)*. Miss Verdun, have you forgotten that dance the other night? I *never* shall.

KITTY. No.

JACK. No! Those stolen moments in the garden by ourselves were the very happiest of all my life, and out there in the moonlight—ah, moonlight is the true atmosphere for—for sentiment.

KITTY. I wonder how many people have said that?

JACK *(let down a little)*. Kitty, I know when you like

you can be an awful plague, but to-day you are quite cynical.

KITTY. I know I am; I'm thinking of that man.

JACK. Of what man?

KITTY. Of my guardian—Mr. Spettigue, who hurries us away from all our best friends directly we get to know anyone really well, for fear of—

JACK. For fear of what?

KITTY (evasively). Oh, I don't know!

JACK. Why *does* he?

KITTY (looking up and smiling). Because he's a selfish, wicked old man.

JACK. Are you—really—so sorry to go away?

KITTY. No, I am angry. But don't speak about it any more, or, as Amy says, "I shall cry."

AMY (rising and speaking to CHARLEY as they come down L. a little). What a dear—sweet—old lady your aunt must be, Mr. Wykeham! I am longing to know her. Where is she?

CHARLEY (aside). Jack! (Rapidly. In agonized aside and beckoning JACK, who goes R.C. to him.) Where's my aunt?

(JACK whispers something in his ear and turns away.)

(Not catching it.) What?

(JACK shrugs shoulders hopelessly and returns to KITTY. KITTY and AMY see nothing of this last scene, which must be played rapidly.)

CHARLEY (to AMY, hesitatingly). Oh, why, she's hardly arrived yet.

AMY (surprised). No, oh! (Crosses to KITTY.) Kitty, Mr. Wykeham's aunt hasn't come yet.

KITTY (rising). Hasn't come? (Crossing to C.) Oh—(Turning to JACK.) Then we must—we'll—run and do some shopping—and come back. Shan't be long. Good-bye!

(KITTY *crosses* AMY *to* L.I.E. CHARLEY *has worked round to door, which he opens.* JACK *follows.*)

AMY *(to* JACK*)*. Good-bye.
JACK. Good-bye.
KITTY *(to* CHARLEY *at door)*. Good-bye.
AMY *(to* CHARLEY *at door—rather sadly)*. Good-bye.

(Exit L.I.E., KITTY *first, then* AMY*.)*

CHARLEY *(at door* L.I.E.*)*. Good-bye! *(Unconsciously taking the same tone.)*

(Slight pause. JACK *and* CHARLEY *look at each other blankly, both sit on* C. *table and shake hands.)*

JACK. See that? Off like a shot when they found your aunt wasn't here.
CHARLEY. Makes an awful difference, doesn't it?
JACK *(hurrying* CHARLEY *off* L.I.E.*)*. Now look here, you cut off to the station and bundle the old girl here in a fly.

*(*CHARLEY *picks up his hat from* C. *table.)*

CHARLEY *(turning at door* L.I.E.*)*. The old girl! What do you mean?
JACK. Well, your aunt—and I'll see after the lunch and keep an eye on Babbs.
CHARLEY *(going)*. All right! *(Returning.)* I say, Jack, I feel happier since I've seen them, don't you?
JACK *(impatiently)*. Yes. Be off! *(Going towards writing-table.)*

(Exit CHARLEY, L.I.E. *Enter* LORD FANCOURT *in shirt-sleeves and waistcoat,* L.U.E., *comes down* L. *of* JACK *cautiously.* JACK *turns and sees* LORD FANCOURT*.)*

LORD FANCOURT. I say, old chap, have you got any hairpins?

(Enter BRASSETT, *L.U.E., coming down L. to sideboard.)*

JACK. Hairpins? Great Scot, no!

LORD FANCOURT. May I send your man for some?

JACK. Yes, certainly.

LORD FANCOURT *(aside to* JACK). I say, have you got sixpence?

JACK *(feeling hurriedly and impatiently in pockets).* No—afraid not.

LORD FANCOURT. Why, you haven't got anything! *(Aside to* BRASSETT.) I say, Brassett, I gave you half-a-crown just now; do you mind making it two shillings and getting me sixpennyworth of hairpins?

BRASSETT *(with a look).* Certainly, m'lord.

LORD FANCOURT. You can keep the change.

(Exit BRASSETT, *L.I.E.)*

I say, Jack, were those the girls?

(Both C.)

JACK. Yes. But what the deuce made you jump out like that? They might have seen you!

LORD FANCOURT. I didn't know they were here.

(Knock at outer door, L.I.E.)

JACK. Look out! There's somebody else.

*(*LORD FANCOURT *bolts and exits door* L.U.E.)*

By George! There was a lot of hope in what Kitty said, in another minute I'd have told her that I— *(Going to table* R., *back turned to door* L.I.E.) But never mind, everything's going on splendidly.

(Knock repeated.)

Come in!

(Enter SIR FRANCIS CHESNEY *L.I.E.)*

(COLONEL SIR FRANCIS CHESNEY, BART., *late Indian Service. Tall, good-looking, smart in appearance and manners, wears small military moustache, actually fifty-one, but looking nearer forty, very smart, cheery and young in manner. Wears brown lounge suit, bowler hat and carries gloves and Malacca walking-stick. He has just arrived from London.)*

SIR FRANCIS. Jack!
JACK *(turning, surprised, and delighted).* Dad!
(Going C.)
SIR FRANCIS. My dear boy!

(They shake hands C.)

JACK. Dear old dad! What brings you here? Wherever have you come from?
SIR FRANCIS. From town, my lad. To have a chat with you and to bring you your checque. *(Puts hat, stick and gloves on sideboard.)*
JACK. Thanks, dad; you're a brick!
SIR FRANCIS *(smiling).* A bit over-baked, my boy; after all my years in India. *(Coming* C. *below table.)*
JACK. A bit crisped, dad, but a humbug pictorially.
SIR FRANCIS. Am I? How do you make that out?
JACK. How old are you?
SIR FRANCIS. What do you say to fifty—
JACK. Fifty?
SIR FRANCIS. *One!*
JACK. Who'd believe it?

SIR FRANCIS. And you, Jack, seem much older than I was at your age— I suppose it's the times—even the old College shows it; new ivy, new paint. *(Looking towards window* C. *Below* C. *table.)*

(Both C., *backs to audience, looking at college through window.)*

JACK. Alma mater's an old beauty still, dad.

(They turn, facing audience again.)

SIR FRANCIS. I suppose she is, by aid of the gentle artifices of the toilet. *(Cheerfully and unconcernedly.)* Well, we all grow old. *(Sits on* C. *table.)*

(SIR FRANCIS takes out pocket-book containing cheque already made out to JACK, and bundle of bills pinned together, with one very long one among them.)

JACK. And as presentably as possible. Why, dear old dad, even you at fifty—
SIR FRANCIS. *One!*
JACK. Fifty years ago would have been a stout, white-haired—or bald—top-booted, domineering old boy! And instead, here you are, a smart, bang up-to date sort of chap one can talk to like a chum! Now how have you done it?
SIR FRANCIS. Don't know.
JACK. Do you drink?
SIR FRANCIS. All I want.
JACK. Eat well?
SIR FRANCIS. Never noticed.
JACK. There you are! Consequently health good, temper perfect—we're going to be great pals, dad.
SIR FRANCIS *(handing cheque)*. Here you are, my boy. There's your cheque to go on with. *(Gives cheque. Looking at bills.)*

JACK. Thanks, dad! *(Sees amount of cheque—smiles to* SIR FRANCIS.) I haven't seen half enough of you.

SIR FRANCIS *(holding up bills).* I see your hospitality—

JACK. I hope, dad—

SIR FRANCIS. Never mind; same when I was a lad.

JACK *(looking at long bill).* I've been done over that wine *monstrously.*

SIR FRANCIS. Were you? Never mind, so was I.

(They laugh. SIR FRANCIS *rises; they both move towards table* R.)

Done over everything monstrously at college, but settle up, settle up—

(JACK *back of table.* SIR FRANCIS L. *of it.)*

I'm very satisfied with you. It's something to go down from college with a record like yours. *(Picks up cigar box and opens it.)* I say, my boy, where the deuce did you get these cigars?

JACK *(casually).* Those, dad?

SIR FRANCIS *(putting box down, sits* L. *by writing-table).* Ah! That accounts for the bills. And now, my lad, we must begin to think.

JACK *(sits at writing-table).* Think?

SIR FRANCIS. Now that I have come into the family title, as you know, I have also—which you don't know—come into the family debts and difficulties.

JACK. Debts!

SIR FRANCIS. Which are far more than I expected, with the result that all the money I've been saving for you in India goes to pay them. And in short, Jack, you and I, for the next few years— will be, comparatively speaking, *poor men.*

JACK *(rises and crosses behind desk to* C.) *Poor* men! *(Aside.)* This settles me with old Spettigue!

Sir Francis *(rising)*. However, I'm in hopes of a small appointment for you—

(Jack *turns hopefully.*)

—in Bengal. *(Goes to fireplace.)*

(Re-enter Brassett, l.i.e.)

Jack. Bengal! What a horrible place! *(Turns, sees* Brassett *as he passes upstage* l., *to him, irritably.)* What is it, Brassett?

Brassett *(holding up, by a fine string loop, a tiny brown paper packet; aside to* Jack). His lordship's hairpins, sir.

Jack. Confound his hairpins!

(Brassett *exits* l.u.e.)

(Aside, recollecting.) By George! The dad'll be an odd one. I must get rid of Babbs somehow if the dad stays. *(Suddenly.)* Stays! Why not? *(Aloud.)* Dad, I've an idea.

(Sir Francis *turns and comes* c. *to* Jack.)

Couldn't this matter be settled by a wealthy marriage?

Sir Francis. No; that's the sort of thing I rather deprecate. I don't think, Jack, I'd—

Jack. Listen. My chum—that is Charley Wykeham's aunt, Donna Lucia d'Alvadorez, is coming here to lunch to-day. She's a widow—

Sir Francis *(dubiously)*. A widow?

Jack. And a millionaire.

Sir Francis *(more hopefully)*. And a millionaire?

Jack. And a *charming* woman.

Sir Francis. No, Jack, I don't think I'd advise you to do a thing of this kind merely for the sake of money.

Jack. No, not me, dad—*you.*

SIR FRANCIS. Me! You young rascal. *(Attempts to punch* JACK.)

(JACK *dodges under his upraised arm to fireplace* R.)

No, no! I shall never marry again. *(Goes towards sideboard.)*

JACK *(bringing him back again* C. *by the arm).* Don't be rash, dad. Think it over. Where are your things?

SIR FRANCIS. At the hotel.

JACK. Go and change. Make yourself look as nice as possible, come back to lunch at one o'clock; and dad, put a flower in your buttonhole—

CHARLEY *(shouting off, excitedly).* I say, Jack!

(Enter CHARLEY, L.I.E., *hurriedly, with telegram. Almost runs into* SIR FRANCIS.)

JACK *(introducing).* Oh, dad, Charley Wykeham. Charley, my father.

SIR FRANCIS *(shakes hands with* CHARLEY). Glad to know you, my boy, glad to know you.

JACK *(to* SIR FRANCIS, *aside).* Her nephew—nice boy, you'll like him.

SIR FRANCIS *(laughing to* CHARLEY). I thought it was the fire brigade.

*(*CHARLEY *laughs, goes up* L. *behind table* C. *to fireplace.)*

JACK. Now, don't forget. Put a flower in your buttonhole, takes years off a man, a flower in his buttonhole.

SIR FRANCIS *(turning and taking hat, stick and gloves from sideboard).* No, Jack, you come and lunch with me at the Mitre. *(At door* L.I.E.)

JACK (C.). Now, don't be rash, dad! See her first, see her *first!*

SIR FRANCIS *(putting his hat on jauntily).* All right,

Jack. I'll have a look at her. *(Smiling.)* I'll have a look at her.

(Exits, L.I.E.)

Jack (c., *to* Charley). Well, what is it?

Charley *(comes down* R. *of* Jack, C.; *excited and anxious; gives telegram).* Read that.

Jack *(reads).* "Important business, don't expect me for a few days. Lucia d'Alvadorez." *(Excitedly.)* No! ! !

Charley *(nervously).* She's not coming!

Jack. But she must! Go—wire—telegraph—

Charley. No use. There's no time. *(Goes up to window* R.)

Jack *(in front of* c. *table).* But hang it! The girls won't remain without a chaperone. What are we to do?

Charley. Couldn't we ask the Proctor's wife, old Mrs.—? *(Looks out of window.)*

Jack *(gloomily).* Who'd sit and stare like an owl.

Charley *(turning—to* Jack). Here they are! *They're* coming! *(Again looking out of window.)*

Jack *(sitting on table* c.). What on earth are we to do?

Lord Fancourt *(off,* L.U.E.). I say, Jack, come and look at me!

Jack *(irritably, turning upstage and going* L.U.E.). What the deuce is it? *(Opens door, looks off, starts back a step in amazement).* By George! Splendid! *(To* Charley.) Charley, come here quickly! Do you know what a pious fraud is?

*(*Charley *crosses to* Jack *up* c.)*

Charley *(surprised and puzzled).* Pious fraud?

Jack. First cousin to a miracle! *(Pushes* Charley *across him.)* Look!

Charley *(looks off* L.U.E.). What is it?

Jack. Babbs—*your aunt!*

CHARLEY. Babbs! *(Turning upon JACK.)* My aunt!

JACK. It's the only one you've got, so you'll have to make the best of her. *(Pushes CHARLEY down to R. Drops down L.)*

LORD FANCOURT *(off)*. I say—look here—

(Enter LORD FANCOURT, dressed as an old lady, L.U.E., in black satin, fichu, wig, cap, etc. Stands up L.C., smiling.)

How's this? *(Then walks down L., smiling benignly.)*

(CHARLEY looks on in amazement. JACK with determined satisfaction. As laughter subsides, JACK speaks.)

JACK. Splendid!

(Loud knock, outer door, L.I.E.)

LORD FANCOURT *(looking at door in affright)*. Who's that? *(Offers to bolt.)*

JACK *(seizing him by the shoulders. L.)*. The girls!

(CHARLEY, R. of LORD FANCOURT.)

LORD FANCOURT *(looking at JACK)*. The girls?

JACK. Charley's aunt can't come.

LORD FANCOURT. Can't she? I'll go and take these things off. *(Turns to bolt up L.U.E.)*

(JACK grabs him, assisted by CHARLEY.)

JACK. No, They won't stop if you do.

LORD FANCOURT. Won't stop! What do you mean?

JACK. You must be Charley's aunt!

LORD FANCOURT *(in dismay)*. Me? *No! ! ! !*

(CHARLEY seizes LORD FANCOURT by R. arm, JACK

holding his L. arm. LORD FANCOURT backs a little and sinks down. They then slide him across to chair L. of writing-table. LORD FANCOURT rises twice and each time is pushed down again by CHARLEY, who then gives chair a kick backwards with the heel of his R. foot, careful to kick chair while it appears to audience as if he had kicked LORD FANCOURT, who writhes. JACK leaves him and gets C. to meet girls. CHARLEY stands L. of the chair so as to hide LORD FANCOURT from door L.I.E. BRASSETT enters, L.U.E.)

JACK. Show them in, Brassett.

(BRASSETT opens door L.I.E. Enter KITTY and AMY, L.I.E. AMY carrying bunch of flowers in tissue paper. JACK joins them. LORD FANCOURT makes an arch of CHARLEY'S right arm, and looks through it to see what girls are like, much to CHARLEY'S annoyance. CHARLEY, furious, smacks LORD FANCOURT'S face (he actually hits his own arm). LORD FANCOURT draws back as though his face had been hit, clamping his hand over his nose and mouth.)

Ah! You've got back. So glad!

(BRASSETT exits, L.U.E.)

KITTY. Yes; we've been longer than we intended, but Amy wanted to get some flowers for Charley's aunt. Has she come?

AMY. Yes. Has she? I hope she's come?

JACK. Oh yes, she's come.

(JACK crosses R.C. KITTY and AMY follow—CHARLEY moves upstage to clear LORD FANCOURT.)

(Introducing.) Donna Lucia, Miss Spettigue, Miss Verdun. *(To girls.)* Donna Lucia d'Alvadorez, Charley's aunt.

(CHARLEY *moves up* R. *a little.* JACK *crosses rapidly behind* LORD FANCOURT, *stands* R. *of him. Slight pause.*)

JACK *(aside to* LORD FANCOURT). Go on, say something!

LORD FANCOURT *(stares at them blankly, and, after a pause).* How do you do, my dears?

KITTY. We called upon you before, Donna Lucia, but you hadn't arrived.

AMY *(crossing* KITTY, *goes to* LORD FANCOURT, *and giving flowers).* And we've brought you these.

LORD FANCOURT *(taking flowers).* Oh, thank you!

(AMY *joins* CHARLEY. *They move up* R.C.)

KITTY. I hope your journey from town hasn't tired you.

LORD FANCOURT. Oh no! It was very jolly.

(JACK *prods him.*)

Pleasant, I mean.

(KITTY *goes up* R.C. *to* AMY *and* CHARLEY.)

(Aside to JACK, *holding up flowers.)* What the deuce am I to do with these things?

JACK *(aside to* LORD FANCOURT). Stick 'em in your dress.

(Bus: LORD FANCOURT *puts flowers in dress, tries to see over them, can't, so parts them and peers between.* BRASSETT *enters,* L.U.E., *comes down* C. *to speak to* LORD FANCOURT, *sees flowers, can't speak.* LORD FANCOURT *winks at him.* BRASSETT *nearly explodes and turns to sideboard hurriedly.)*

AMY *(at back of table* C. *To* CHARLEY). You look worried, Mr. Wykeham. Are you ill?

CHARLEY. No; I'm anxious, I'm—

JACK *(coming to the rescue)*. He's a little affected at meeting his aunt to-day for the first time. *(Aside to* LORD FANCOURT, *prodding him.)* Why the dickens don't you say something?

LORD FANCOURT. What the dickens am I to say?

JACK. Talk about the weather.

LORD FANCOURT *(aloud to girls.)* Charming weather.

KITTY. Oh, yes, delightful!   ⎫
AMY. Oh, yes, it is charming!⎬ *(Together.)*

BRASSETT *(at door,* L.I.E.). Well, College gents'll do anything!

(BRASSETT exits, L.I.E.)

LORD FANCOURT *(aside to* JACK). You know, you're placing me in a terribly false position.

AMY *(coming down* R. *to* LORD FANCOURT). May I arrange these for you, Donna Lucia?

(LORD FANCOURT takes flowers out of dress and hands her them.)

After all, you know, we have some nice weather sometimes in poor old England.

(Turns to CHARLEY, *then joins* KITTY *at* C. *table.* CHARLEY *then goes* L. *of* LORD FANCOURT.)*

LORD FANCOURT *(aside to* JACK). What on earth does she mean by that?

JACK. Why, you're a foreigner.

LORD FANCOURT. A foreigner! What did you say my name was?

JACK. Donna Lucia d'Alvadorez.

LORD FANCOURT. What am I? Irish?

CHARLEY (L. *side of him*). No, English. Married a Portuguese abroad.

JACK. A widow.

CHARLEY. From Brazil.

JACK. And a millionaire.

LORD FANCOURT (*to* CHARLEY). I say, Charley, have I any children?

CHARLEY. No, you fool!

(CHARLEY *kicks chair as before.* LORD FANCOURT *hurriedly rubs leg as though hurt.* BRASSETT *enters with tray, places it on* C. *table arranges the luncheon things, standing* C. *below table, back to audience.* KITTY *and* AMY *help during the following scene.* BRASSETT *also arranges three single chairs, two behind one end of table* L.)

LORD FANCOURT. Well, one ought to know. That's all right. Now I can go ahead. Yes, it is wonderful weather, for England.

KITTY. Yes, it is. } (*Together, a little puzzled*).
AMY. Yes. }

LORD FANCOURT (*aside to* JACK, *rising*). Shall I take them to see the chapel and the cloisters?

(JACK *and* CHARLEY *pull him back violently in the chair.*)

JACK. No; you leave that to me and Charley; we'll attend to them.

KITTY (*coming down* L. *of table* C. *to* LORD FANCOURT). Of course, Oxford is all very new to you, Donna Lucia, but it's a dear old place in any weather. Amy and I will show you all about.

LORD FANCOURT. I shall be delighted. (*Rises.*)

(*They push him back as before.*)

KITTY (*to* LORD FANCOURT *again*). You're staying till to-morrow, are you not?

LORD FANCOURT (*aside to* JACK). Am I staying until to-morrow?

JACK (*quickly and rather loudly*). No.

LORD FANCOURT *(quickly and very loudly)*. No.

(The girls turn round in surprise.)

KITTY. Oh. *(Returns to* L. *of table* C., *helps to lay lunch.)*

AMY. Oh, but you will, you must! *(To* KITTY.) Mustn't she, Kitty?

CHARLEY *(anxiously)*. I'm afraid auntie can't stay after to-day.

*(*KITTY *joins* AMY *up* C.)

LORD FANCOURT. No; you see, it's my washing day. *(Crosses legs.)*

*(*CHARLEY, *who is standing* L. *of him, pushes* LORD FANCOURT'S *knee down again.)*

CHARLEY *(to girls, explaining)*. She has so much business to attend to—in town. *(Joining girls up* R.C.)

JACK. Yes, lawyers, stocks—

LORD FANCOURT. Yes, stocks and socks—

*(*JACK *punches him.)*

—all very important, you know.

*(*AMY *comes down* L. *of* LORD FANCOURT.)

AMY. Oh, I'm so sorry, we have so longed to know you.

LORD FANCOURT. Have you, my dear? *(Takes* AMY'S *hand.)*

AMY *(standing by* LORD FANCOURT). Mr. Wykeham has told us so much about you, that he has made us quite love you.

*(*KITTY *sits* R. *corner of window seat.* CHARLEY *comes down behind* AMY.)

LORD FANCOURT *(slipping his L. arm round* AMY's *waist)*. Has he, my dear?

(CHARLEY *takes* LORD FANCOURT'S *arm away angrily.* LORD FANCOURT *replaces it,* CHARLEY *pulls it away again.* AMY *kneels.* LORD FANCOURT *slips his arm round her shoulders and gives her a quick little hug, and both the boys a look of triumph.* CHARLEY *furious, crosses to* L.; *goes up, knocks off cap from figure up* L., *returns down* L. *and sulks.)*

AMY *(kneeling by* LORD FANCOURT). And he's so grateful; he says he owes *everything* to you and never could repay you, and oh, he is such a good frank, upright man—it was noble of you!

LORD FANCOURT. Of course, my dear *(taking his arm from round her, quietly)* it was only my duty to see after the welfare of my poor brother's—

JACK *(aside to* LORD FANCOURT, *quickly)*. Sister's, you fool!

LORD FANCOURT *(to* AMY, *repeating)*. Sister's, you fool— *(correcting himself)* sister's *(with aggressive look at* JACK) and *(to* AMY) brother-in-law's orphan girl.

JACK *(aside, as before)*. Boy! Boy!

LORD FANCOURT *(to* AMY). Boy—boy! *(Aside to* JACK.) I'll say twins in a minute.

(BRASSETT, *below table, back to audience, has during this scene been laying luncheon, now exits* L.I.E.)

AMY. Yes, but it was so good of you to find out; you were so far away in a foreign land, and he might have been left to starve, or to fall into cruel hands. But you have a good, kind, affectionate nature—

LORD FANCOURT. Have I, my dear?

AMY. Anyone can see it in your face.

LORD FANCOURT. No!

AMY. I feel I could tell my whole heart to you! *(Looks away to* CHARLEY, L.)

JACK *(to* LORD FANCOURT, *aside).* Don't let her.

LORD FANCOURT *(aside to* JACK). I'm not going to. The dear little thing!

AMY *(to* LORD FANCOURT). You don't mind my talking to you like this, do you?

LORD FANCOURT. My dear, you are a very charming little girl, of whom I am sure I could soon grow very fond— *(Looks over* AMY'S *head at* CHARLEY *and waves.)*

(CHARLEY *shakes fist at him.)*

And you must tell me all you like, some day, when you know me better.

(AMY *again looks away to* CHARLEY L.)

(Aside to JACK.) How the devil is that?

AMY. Oh, *(rises)* I feel I've known you years and years already.

(Kisses LORD FANCOURT *and joins* KITTY *in window, sits* L. *corner.* CHARLEY *flies at* LORD FANCOURT, *punching him viciously.* JACK *same. Bus. on other side, then both join girls at window.)*

LORD FANCOURT *(aside).* They're jealous! I'm very sorry, but it was very nice.

(Enter BRASSETT L.I.E., *hurriedly to* L.C.)

BRASSETT *(to* JACK, *in an anxious manner, and half aside).* Mr. Chesney! Mr. Chesney!

(JACK *comes down to* BRASSETT.)

I beg pardon, sir, but I heard Mr. Spettigue enquiring at the gate for your rooms, sir.

AMY *and* KITTY. Oh dear, my uncle⎫
back!   ⎬ *(together).*
CHARLEY. Mr. Spettigue!   ⎭

(All rise, general consternation. All remain above C. *table.)*

JACK *(aghast).* Mr. Spettigue back! I thought he was in London. *(Returning to others above table.)*

(BRASSETT *goes up* L., *draws curtains of recess.)*

KITTY. Mr. Chesney, I beg of you to send him away.

(Knock L.I.E. *on outer door.* KITTY, AMY *and* JACK *exit into recess* L.C. BRASSETT *exits* L.U.E. LORD FANCOURT *looks scared at knock, and bolts to window* R.C., *leaps on to window-seat about to get out.* CHARLEY *turns bolts after him, seizes him round waist as he is getting through window, carries him downstage,* LORD FANCOURT'S *feet, with soles showing to audience spread out,* CHARLEY *plumps him down* R.C. *front.)*

LORD FANCOURT *(in terror, grabbing* CHARLEY). What am I to say? What am I to do?
CHARLEY. Stay where you are, Babbs. Tell him what you like, only get rid of him.

(CHARLEY *exits quickly through curtains into recess.* LORD FANCOURT *stands* R.C. *Knock again, louder.)*

SPETTIGUE *(off; in a loud and angry voice).* Why doesn't somebody answer this door?

(STEPHEN SPETTIGUE *is a well-to-do solicitor of about fifty-six to sixty. Rather stout and when not in a temper has a charming smile, so that in spite of everything you can't help liking him. He has real charm of*

*manner when he likes to use it. At other times, he is
pompous, self-opinionated, assertive, and not open
to argument. He is grey-haired, and can be rather
bald—wears small short side whiskers a la Sir Ed-
ward Clarke. Dressed in a frock-coat, grey cloth
waistcoat, wearing top-hat, and carrying furled um-
brella, and gloves.*

*This character should not be burlesqued; he is
genuinely furious, but when he is charming, he knows
how to make that too seem genuine.*

Enter SPETTIGUE, *angrily, with hat on,* L.I.E., *cross-
in to* LORD FANCOURT.)

SPETTIGUE. Why doesn't somebody answer this door?

LORD FANCOURT *(fixing him aggressively and backing
him across stage to* L.C., *then suddenly to him, loudly).*
What do you want?

SPETTIGUE. I wish to see Mr. Chesney.

LORD FANCOURT *(Pointing with closed fan).* Where
did you get that hat? *(Aggressively.)* Take it off, sir!
(Moving away a little to C.)

(SPETTIGUE *removes hat, goes to table and is about to
sit chair* L. *of table* C.)

Don't sit down, sir!

(SPETTIGUE *straightens hurriedly.)*

I'm not sitting down. I didn't ask you to sit down.

SPETTIGUE *(coming down a little).* We'll waive that
for the present, madam. I wish to see Mr. Chesney at
once.

LORD FANCOURT. Well, you can't see him; he's not
present. I am the only person present.

SPETTIGUE. But the porter told me that two young
ladies—my niece and my ward—were here.

LORD FANCOURT. I tell you I am the only young
lady present.

SPETTIGUE (c.). But he told me he saw them come in. *(Taps top of hat.)*

LORD FANCOURT. And didn't he tell you he saw them go out? *(Taps hat twice with last two words, with fan.)*

SPETTIGUE *(loudly)*. No!

LORD FANCOURT *(just as loudly)*. Very well then, what more do you want?

SPETTIGUE. They've gone into the garden. *(Turning upstage, towards recess.)*

LORD FANCOURT *(turning with him up R.C.)*. They've done nothing of the kind.

SPETTIGUE *(coming down L.C. again)*. Then they've gone into the town. *(Going towards door L.I.E.)*

LORD FANCOURT *(coming down R.C.)*. Well, why couldn't you think of that before? *(Crossing to SPETTIGUE.)* And now, sir, having got all the information you are likely to get, in your present condition— *(eyeing him all over).*

SPETTIGUE. Madam!

LORD FANCOURT. Disgraceful! Where have you been? *(Moving away a little to c.)*

SPETTIGUE *(following)*. What do you mean, madam? I am annoyed, but perfectly sober.

LORD FANCOURT. Well, you don't look it. *(Moving to side of writing-table R.C.)* Other people can be annoyed as well as yourself. *(Sits chair L. of it and picks up time-table or other light book.)*

SPETTIGUE. Madam, I apologise. Good morning. *(Puts his hat on, turns and goes towards L.I.E.)*

(As he turns to go, LORD FANCOURT half rises, throws book, knocks SPETTIGUE's hat off, then sits again chair L. of table R., assuming an unconscious air.

This business is done by SPETTIGUE putting his hat on lightly and slightly on one side. LORD FANCOURT holds A.B.C. in flat of right hand, and half propels it out of his hand with an upward movement, catching the right side of hat, and so sending the hat upstage. Done otherwise at any other angle,

there is a danger of the brim of the hat hitting SPET-
TIGUE'S *nose.)*

(Retrieves hat, pointing to it.) Did you see anything
strike that hat?

LORD FANCOURT. I beg your pardon?

SPETTIGUE. Did you see anything strike that hat?
(Putting hat closer to him.)

LORD FANCOURT *(aside)*. He wants me to do it again.
(Strikes hat with fan.)

(SPETTIGUE *puts on hat and exits* L.I.E., *angrily.)*

(Going up R. *towards recess, calling to girls.)* Oh, my
dears!

(Re-enter KITTY *and* AMY, *followed by* JACK *and*
CHARLEY.)

KITTY *(to* LORD FANCOURT, *up* R.C.). It was sweet
of you!

AMY. You darling!

(One on each side of LORD FANCOURT, *they kiss him.)*

CHARLEY *(up* L.). Look at him, Jack!

JACK *(up* L.C.). I'll punch his head if he does it
again!

(Knock. BRASSETT *enters,* L.U.E.)

(To CHARLEY.) Here's my father! *(Going down* C. *To*
LORD FANCOURT.) Donna Lucia!

(LORD FANCOURT comes down C. *to* JACK. CHARLEY
joins girls up R.C.)

(Aside to LORD FANCOURT.) Take care, here's my
father.

LORD FANCOURT. Look here, am I any relation to him?

JACK. No; you're *Charley's* Aunt, from Brazil.

LORD FANCOURT. Brazil! Where's that?

JACK. You know—er—where the nuts come from.

(LORD FANCOURT *is hurried on to chair* L. *of writing table.* CHARLEY *goes down* L. *of* LORD FANCOURT, *screening him from door as before.* JACK C. BRASSETT *opens door* L.I.E. *for* SIR FRANCIS CHESNEY *and waits to take his hat and stick. Enter* SIR FRANCIS CHESNEY. *He has changed into frock coat, silk hat, stick and carries gloves, and wears a deep cerise-red carnation.* KITTY *and* AMY *up* R.C.)

JACK *(introducing—to* KITTY). Miss Verdun, my father.

SIR FRANCIS. Delighted.

JACK *(to* AMY). Miss Spettigue, my father.

(KITTY *and* AMY *bow.)*

SIR FRANCIS. Charmed. *(Turns, sees* BRASSETT.)

(BRASSETT *takes his hat and stick and places them on hat-rack in recess. Exits.)*

(To BRASSETT.) Thank you. *(Aside, to* JACK.) Now, Jack, has she come?

JACK. Oh yes, she's come. *(Crossing to* CHARLEY—*aside.)* Go on, Charley, introduce your aunt.

CHARLEY *(to* LORD FANCOURT). Donna Lucia d' Alvadorez, Sir Francis Chesney, Jack's father.

(SIR FRANCIS *stares at* LORD FANCOURT.)

LORD FANCOURT. How do you do, Sir Francis?

SIR FRANCIS. How do you do? *(Blankly.)*

LORD FANCOURT. I'm Charley's aunt from Brazil—where the nuts come from.

(CHARLEY *gets before chair and kicks as before, goes upstage and joins ladies in window.* LORD FANCOURT *holds his leg in pain.*)

SIR FRANCIS *(aside to* JACK*).* I say, Jack!
JACK *(goes quickly to him).* Yes?
SIR FRANCIS. Is *that* the lady?
JACK. Eh? Yes.

(SIR FRANCIS *points to flower in his buttonhole.)*

Yes.
SIR FRANCIS *(blankly).* Oh, by George! *(Turns towards door,* L.I.E.*)*
JACK *(catching his arm to stop him).* Oh, don't go, dad! *(Then crosses rapidly to* LORD FANCOURT. *Aside, hurriedly.)* Go on, Charley's told you all about him. *(Goes* R. *of* LORD FANCOURT.*)*
LORD FANCOURT *(repeating like a parrot; to* SIR FRANCIS*).* Charley's told you all about him.
JACK *(whispering.)* No, no!
LORD FANCOURT *(to* SIR FRANCIS*).* No, no!
JACK *(whispering and prompting him).* My nephew Charles.
LORD FANCOURT *(to* SIR FRANCIS*).* My nephew Charles has told me so much about you—
JACK *(with a prod—aside).* —in his letters—
LORD FANCOURT. In his letters—in his letters— *(Aside to* JACK.*)* That's all right, isn't it?
JACK *(viciously).* No, it isn't.
LORD FANCOURT. Do it yourself! *(Looks sulky.)*

(JACK *moves* L. *of* LORD FANCOURT.*)*

SIR FRANCIS. I'm much obliged to Mr. Wykeham, but I only met him to-day for the first time.
JACK *(aside to* LORD FANCOURT*).* See! *(Aloud to* SIR FRANCIS.*)* Yes, but dad, I've been simply photographing you to Charley for years.

LORD FANCOURT *(to* SIR FRANCIS, *brightening).* Oh yes, he's a splendid photographer!

JACK *(aside to* LORD FANCOURT). Remember you've only just come to England, and you've never seen Charley till to-day.

LORD FANCOURT. Why the deuce didn't you say so before?

(Re-enter BRASSETT *from recess* L.C.)

SIR FRANCIS. Jack!

*(*JACK *comes quickly to* SIR FRANCIS, C.)

(Aside to JACK.) My dear boy, it's impossible!

JACK. What, dad?

SIR FRANCIS *(with a look towards* LORD FANCOURT). Well—*look* at her!

JACK. Eh? *(Suddenly remembering his suggestion of marriage.)* Oh, good gracious!

BRASSETT. Luncheon is ready, sir. *(Takes dish cover to sideboard.)*

*(*CHARLEY *brings* AMY *and* KITTY *to luncheon table* C., AMY L. CHARLEY *stands* L., *upper corner of* C. *table.* KITTY *top* L.)

JACK *(crossing to* LORD FANCOURT—*aside).* Take my father, and be careful how you talk to him. *(To* SIR FRANCIS.) Dad, will you take Donna Lucia? *(Goes to* R. *corner of table* C., *taking chair from* R. *end.)*

SIR FRANCIS *(offering arm to* LORD FANCOURT). Allow me, Donna Lucia.

*(*LORD FANCOURT *rises, takes* SIR FRANCIS's *arm and they move up to table.)*

LORD FANCOURT. You'll sit beside me, won't you, Sir Francis?

(SIR FRANCIS *takes chair from* L. *end of writing-table, places it at* R. *end of* C. *table for* LORD FAN-COURT, *who sits.* BRASSETT *gets chair from below door* L.I.E., *places it below* C. *table for* SIR FRAN-CIS. *They all sit.*)

SIR FRANCIS. I shall be delighted. (*Sits* C., *back to audience.*) You've travelled a great deal, I suppose?

LORD FANCOURT. Oh yes, I've been a great traveller, Sir Francis. I came all the way from London only this morning.

(BRASSETT *looking about for champagne through this scene.*)

CHARLEY (*serving mayonnaise*). Donna Lucia— Aunt— (*louder*) Aunt!

(JACK *prods him.*)

—mayonnaise?

LORD FANCOURT (*sweetly*). Thank you.

CHARLEY. Miss Spettigue—

AMY. Yes, please.

CHARLEY. Miss Verdun?

KITTY. Please.

LORD FANCOURT (*to* SIR FRANCIS). What a pretty flower!

SIR FRANCIS. Do you like it? (*Offers it.*) Will you accept it?

LORD FANCOURT. Oh, thank you (*takes flower, holding it out*). I'll have it stuffed. (*Puts it in dress.*)

CHARLEY. Jack, mayonnaise? (*To* BRASSETT.) Open the wine, Brassett.

KITTY (*to* JACK). You have very pleasant rooms here, Mr. Chesney.

(BRASSETT *pours claret into* SIR FRANCIS's *glass and returns to sideboard to watch result.*)

JACK. Oh yes.

AMY. Oh yes, they're awfully nice rooms, Mr. Chesney, I'm sure. Don't you think so, Sir Francis?

SIR FRANCIS. Pleasanter to-day *(with a look from* LORD FANCOURT *to* AMY) than usual, I fancy. Donna Lucia, may I have the pleasure? *(Sip wine, puts glass down in disgust.)* Jack, my boy, where did you get this stuff?

AMY. May I have a little water, please?

JACK *(to* BRASSETT). Open the champagne, Brassett.

BRASSETT. I—I can't find it, sir.

(LORD FANCOURT *laughing to himself.)*

JACK *(rising)*. Can't find it? Do you know where it is, Charley? *(Looking about room, under table, etc.,* R.)

CHARLEY. No. *(Looking in recess up* L.)

JACK *(sternly to* BRASSETT). What's become of it? I thought it was in ice.

LORD FANCOURT *(who has been laughing to himself; taps table with spoon, they all look at him)*. What is it? What is it you want?

JACK. The champagne, Donna Lucia. *(Going up to* LORD FANCOURT.)

LORD FANCOURT. What, haven't you got any? Well, I thought you'd forget something, so I brought some with me in my bag— In my bag, Brassett.

(JACK *punches* LORD FANCOURT. BRASSETT *takes bag off chair up* L. *and goes to sideboard and takes out champagne. Enter* SPETTIGUE L.I.E., *in a rage with hat on.)*

SPETTIGUE. Ah!

AMY *and* KITTY. Uncle!

JACK *and* CHARLEY. Mr. Spettigue! } *(together).*

(All rise except SIR FRANCIS.)

SPETTIGUE *(just inside door* L.I.E.; *sees girls).* So, I was right after all, and that old fool of a woman told me they were not here.

(LORD FANCOURT *and girls come down* R.C. SIR FRAN-CIS *rises, puts chair under table.* JACK, *taking the bull by the horns, coming forward.)*

JACK *(offering his hand, gaily).* Oh, Mr. Spettigue—
SPETTIGUE (L.). Don't address me, sir!

(JACK *falls back a little.)*

(To girls.) And this is the way you take advantage of my absence!

(CHARLEY *up* L. JACK R.C.)

JACK. Mr. Spettigue!
SPETTIGUE. Don't address me, sir! I have no wish to hold any converse with you.
CHARLEY *(coming down a little* L. *of table* C. *between* JACK *and* SPETTIGUE). But won't you allow us to explain?
SPETTIGUE *(pointing to* JACK). My business is with this young man, sir, and not with you.
LORD FANCOURT (R., *coming forward a little).* But you won't listen to either of them!
SPETTIGUE *(insolently).* Go away, madam, and don't interfere.
LORD FANCOURT. Where did you get that hat? Take it off, sir!

(SPETTIGUE *takes off hat, turning.)*

JACK *(coming forward again—to* SPETTIGUE). You forget yourself, sir.
SIR FRANCIS (C., *with quiet tone of authority).* Perhaps you will remember, sir, that ladies are present

SPETTIGUE *(loftily)*. I disapprove of their presence and request them to return with me.

JACK. We can discuss this matter on a more fitting occasion.

LORD FANCOURT. Certainly. A most excellent suggestion. Let him call again.

SPETTIGUE. You're a very foolish old woman, and I must beg of you not to interfere. *(At door.)* Ladies, come!

(KITTY *and* AMY *move forward reluctantly, but* LORD FANCOURT *puts out his arms to bar the way and they each take his arm instead.)*

SIR FRANCIS. Sir, you cannot put such an affront upon Mr. Wykeham's friends.

SPETTIGUE. I don't know them; I don't know them.

SIR FRANCIS *(to* CHARLEY). Introduce me, Mr. Wykeham.

CHARLEY *(drops downstage a little)*. Mr. Spettigue—Sir Francis Chesney. *(Falls back.)*

(SPETTIGUE *barely acknowledges introduction.)*

SIR FRANCIS (C.). Mr. Chesney is my son, sir; and *(turning to* LORD FANCOURT) this lady is—

LORD FANCOURT *(standing between the two girls and effecting to be hurt)*. Pray don't introduce him to me. *I've* been sufficiently insulted by the old boun—er—gentleman—already.

SPETTIGUE. I consult my own feelings when I say that I am deeply annoyed to find on prematurely returning from town, my niece and my ward lunching, without my permission, with these two young gentlemen.

SIR FRANCIS *(firmly)*. To meet Mr. Wykeham's aunt.

SPETTIGUE *(with insulting disbelief)*. Indeed!

SIR FRANCIS *(anger rising)*. There is no "Indeed"

about it, sir! I repeat, to meet Mr. Wykeham's aunt.
SPETTIGUE. In my mind it matters little.
SIR FRANCIS. In my mind it matters everything,
therefore—

(KITTY *and* AMY *let go of* LORD FANCOURT's *arms.*)

—allow me to introduce you. *(To* LORD FANCOURT.)
Donna Lucia d'Alvadorez! Mr.— *(Aside to* JACK.)
What's his confounded name, Jack?
SPETTIGUE *(aside).* Donna Lucia } *(together).*
JACK. Spettigue.   }
SIR FRANCIS *(finishing introduction).* Mr. Spettigue.
SPETTIGUE *(surprised—aside).* The celebrated mil-
lionaire?

(The boys see the change. LORD FANCOURT *crossing
to* SPETTIGUE.)

Oh, how do you do.
LORD FANCOURT. How do you do. I am Charley's
aunt from Brazil, where the nuts come from.

(JACK *pushes* LORD FANCOURT, *who falls against*
SPETTIGUE. LORD FANCOURT *tries to turn the fall
into an awkward curtsy—then turns furiously to*
JACK.)

SPETTIGUE *(aside).* I've been indiscreet. *(To* LORD
FANCOURT.) Oh, I am sorry, very, very sorry.

(CHARLEY *goes up round back of* C. *table, takes* AMY
back to luncheon table: she sits in same place again.)

JACK *(aside to* LORD FANCOURT). Go on, he's apolo-
gised. Ask him to lunch.

(JACK *takes* KITTY *back to luncheon table, same place.*)

LORD FANCOURT (*to* SPETTIGUE). Well, I thought you were very rude, but if you apologise, you know—
SPETTIGUE (*quickly*). Oh, by all means. I am sorry, I am very sorry.
LORD FANCOURT. You'll stay to lunch, won't you?

(BRASSETT *down* L., *takes hat and stick from* SPETTIGUE.)

SPETTIGUE. If *you* wish it—and I am forgiven?
LORD FANCOURT. Forgiven! (*Takes flower from dress.*) Here, accept this as a peace offering. (*Puts* SIR FRANCIS'S *flower into* SPETTIGUE'S *coat.*)

(*Orchestra starts playing curtain music very softly, which swells to full volume as curtain falls.*)

SIR FRANCIS (*down* R.C., *indignantly*). My flower! (*Crosses to* LORD FANCOURT *and* SPETTIGUE.)

(CHARLEY *and* AMY, JACK *and* KITTY *seated as before.*)

(*Offers* L. *arm to* LORD FANCOURT.) Allow me, Donna Lucia.
SPETTIGUE. No, allow me. (*Offers* R. *arm.*)

(LORD FANCOURT *hesitates—flutters eyelashes at them both, then chooses* SPETTIGUE'S *arm. They go towards chair* R. *end of table* C. SIR FRANCIS *leaves them and goes up to chair* R. *of table* C., *which he holds ready for* LORD FANCOURT. SPETTIGUE *offers to take the chair from* SIR FRANCIS, *between the two the chair is drawn back and* LORD FANCOURT *sits on floor. The others rise with screams and exclamations.*)

TABLEAU.

CURTAIN.

ACT TWO

"While there's tea there's hope."—*Pinero.*

SCENE.—*Exterior of* JACK CHESNEY'S *rooms, St. Olde's College, Oxford.*

Housepiece showing part of College, with two casement windows on ground floor and two above, at back with arch R.C. in continuation view of Quad beyond. Door with knocker and name-plate to rooms, running from housepiece and showing through arch. Low wall joining this to arch showing chapel down R. through arch. Continuation of College up L. Window on first floor and small arch beneath running downstage. Arch down L. to garden. Trees R. and L. and meeting overhead. Yellow sunlight, afternoon small round iron table C., with 2 first act chairs R. and L. of it—Victorian wicker or white iron may be substituted if preferred. Rustic chair up C., with cushions. Table L. of it.

Lights full up.

BRASSETT *discovered above table C. with cigarette box, ashtray and match box on salvar, places them on table C.*

BRASSETT. Well, we're sailing along. *(Looks off L.)* He makes a wonderful old lady—not a doubt about it. *(With another look.)* A bit singular to look at, perhaps, but then look at some of your old ladies! Nobody'd believe 'em *possible,* and he don't seem a bit worse to look at than two or three I could mention holding very 'igh positions, too. *(Looks off again.)* Both the old gents have got their eye on her. *(Amused.)* Lor'!—if they only knew. I fancy Sir Francis is favourite, although old Spettigue fancies himself— *(Chuckles loudly—going down* L.) Well, College gents'll do anything! *(Chuckles.)*

(Enter JACK *through arch* R.C., *wearing straw hat, sees* BRASSETT.)

JACK *(coming down in front of table to* BRASSETT, *severely).* What are you laughing at, eh?

BRASSETT. Beg pardon, sir—I was thinking of an old aunt o' mine—

JACK. Eh?

BRASSETT *(respectfully).* Uncle, I mean.

JACK. Mind your own business, and go and get tea—do you see? Tea.

BRASSETT. Tea, sir; yes, sir. *(Goes up to* R.C.)

JACK. Out here. *(Going* L.)

BRASSETT *(turning, surprised).* Out here, sir?

JACK. Yes, don't stare like that, it's all right. I've got special permission.

BRASSETT. Oh, beg pardon, sir.

(Exit through arch R.C. *to rooms.)*

JACK. Well, now for Kitty. Where is she? Everything's going on all right at last. *(Sits* L. *of table* C.) Babbs frightened the life out of me two or three times at lunch, the way he walked into things as if he hadn't had food for a month. But we've got over the worst. *(Looking off* L.) All the same, I haven't been able to have my chat yet with Kitty, but now they're all nicely settled down, I've given her a hint to meet me here, where we can talk quietly—

(Enter CHARLEY *quickly* R.C., *looking off* R. JACK *rises, turns quickly, hearing footsteps.)*

JACK. Here she is!

(Both raise hats, meet c., turn away in disgust.)

Oh, hang it! I've a most particular appointment here with Kitty—so hook it!

CHARLEY. But so have I, Jack.

JACK. With Kitty?

CHARLEY. No, with Amy.

JACK. Then we've both made appointments in the same place. Confound it all, what are we to do?

CHARLEY *(sadly, crossing L.)*. Well, they're your rooms.

JACK *(aggressively)*. Yes, but you're my guest! *(Suddenly and brightly.)* Here, come on *(feels in pocket, has nothing)* we'll toss for it. *(They come c.)* Got any money?

(CHARLEY brings out of pockets—knife, string, a key and a halfpenny.)

CHARLEY. A ha'penny, that's all.

JACK *(takes halfpenny)*. Sudden death. *(Tosses.)* Heads, you and Amy, tails me and— *(Sees KITTY off L.I.E.)* Here she is! *(Pockets coin. Crosses to L.C.)*

CHARLEY *(to JACK)*. Jack, that's all the money I've got! (c.).

(Enter KITTY, L.I.E. CHARLEY looks disgusted and goes R.C.)

KITTY. Oh, Mr. Chesney, there you are.

JACK *(with a look at CHARLEY)*. Yes, I'm here—in fact, waiting— *(Another look at CHARLEY. Aside to KITTY.)* I was beginning to fear you wouldn't come. *(Another look at CHARLEY, then crosses to him.)* Why don't you go? Have you no tact?

(Enter AMY, R.C.)

CHARLEY *(to* JACK, *aside).* But what about me and Amy?

AMY *(coming down* R. *to* CHARLEY). Ah, Mr. Wykeham, *there* you are.

CHARLEY. Yes, I was coming—I was waiting, I'm here. *(Going to* AMY.)

(Bus. of looks, etc., between JACK *and* CHARLEY.)

JACK *(aside).* Beastly awkward. *(With sudden determination.)* Oh, I say, Charley, have you shown Miss Spettigue all round the garden?

CHARLEY *(cloudily).* Yes, Jack, I *have*—two or three times! In fact, we've just come from there. *(Aside to* AMY.) I wish he'd leave us.

JACK *(after a pause—to* AMY). Er—lovely garden, isn't it?

AMY. Yes, I suppose it is.

JACK *(catching at it).* "Suppose?" *(Goes behind* AMY *and* CHARLEY, *taking them by the arm to* L.C.) Oh, you haven't half seen it. Charley, Miss Spettigue hasn't half seen the garden.

*(*KITTY *goes up behind table to arch* R.C., *watching with interest and amusement.)*

Take her and show her the roses and primroses, and cabbages and things.

*(*AMY *wanders up—looks off* L.U.E.)

CHARLEY *(stopping* L.C.). But, Jack, I—

JACK (C.). And, Charley, tell Miss Spettigue those beautiful lines of yours—"To Our Garden In Summer."

CHARLEY *(aside to* JACK, *anxiously).* Jack, don't tell her I write poetry. She'll think I'm an awful ass.

*(*AMY *comes down* L. *again.)*

JACK *(turning L. to* AMY*)*. And don't forget, Miss Spettigue, tea in half an hour.

AMY. Oh, very well, Mr. Chesney.

(Exit slowly, L.I.E.*)*

CHARLEY *(following* AMY, *then turns back. Aside to* JACK*)*. But, Jack, the others are in the garden, and it worries the life out of me to see Babbs.

*(*KITTY *comes down* C. *table, sits* R.*)*

JACK. Well, *don't*. It's a large garden; keep out of his way. *(Pushing* CHARLEY *off* L.I.E.*)*

(Exit CHARLEY, L.I.E.*)*

(Going behind table C. *to* KITTY.*)* At last, Miss Verdun —my dear Kitty—we are alone!

KITTY *(teasing)*. Don't you think it was rather selfish of us, Mr. Chesney, to send them away like that?

JACK. Well, we tossed for it.

KITTY *(turning in mock surprise)*. What?

JACK. I mean—er—they'll be much happier together, *alone:* and it seems as if I could never get five minutes with you safe from some miserable interruption. Indeed, I was beginning to fear you'd think me very rude, neglecting you as I have done. *(Gets* R. *of* KITTY.*)*

KITTY *(an undercurrent of teasing running through all her scene)*. Oh no, not at all, I quite understand. I couldn't expect you to devote yourself *entirely* to me. *(Rising and crossing* L.*)* Indeed we've had a very pleasant time, and now—

JACK. Yes, and now? *(Following her down* R. *of table.)*

KITTY. I was thinking we ought to be going now.

JACK. Go? Now? Good gracious, no!

KITTY *(with elevated eyebrows)*. Why not?

JACK. Before I've had a word with you? *(With en-*

thusiasm.) Oh, my dear Miss Verdun—Kitty— *(Approaching* KITTY *suddenly,* L. *About to put arm round her waist.)*

(KITTY *draws herself up and a little away in surprise, with a look of comic enquiry.* JACK *pulls himself up.)*

Won't you sit down? *(Offers chair* L.C., *then goes behind* C. *table.)* I have something to say to you of importance.

KITTY *(sits* L. *of table* C.). Indeed, Mr. Chesney?

JACK. Yes. *(Moving round* R. *to front of table* C.) You know, Miss Verdun, there are times when a fellow's got to think a lot and think long.

KITTY. I suppose so. *(Putting* R. *hand unconsciously on table.)*

JACK (C.). And there are times when a fellow mustn't stop to think, or if he does, he'll spoil his chance!

KITTY. Yes.

JACK. Well, then, Miss Verdun—Kitty—my dear Kitty— *(About to take her hand.)*

(Enter SIR FRANCIS, L.I.E.)

SIR FRANCIS. Oh, I beg pardon.

(JACK *moves* R., KITTY *rises to go.)*

No, don't mind me. I only wanted a word with my boy here.

KITTY *(to* SIR FRANCIS). Oh, then, I'll run into the garden—

(SIR FRANCIS *crosses behind* C. *table up* R.C.)

(Catches JACK'S *eye; he crosses to her* L.) —and see the roses and primroses, and cabbages and things.

(Exit L.I.E.*)*

JACK *(turning to* C.*)*. Well, dad—anything important?

SIR FRANCIS *(coming down* R.C. *to* JACK, C.*)*. Yes, Jack, it is.

JACK. Oh, what is it?

SIR FRANCIS. You know I'd do anything to see you get on in the world, and make a mark—as I know you will, if you get your chance—

JACK. You needn't tell me all this, dad.

SIR FRANCIS. Well, Jack, having thought it over I've decided that you shall continue the career I originally mapped out for you, and seeing a way out of the difficulty, I've determined to take your advice, my boy, and marry a lady of wealth.

JACK. I see, you've fallen a victim to the fascinations of some young and lovely—

SIR FRANCIS. No, Jack, she's not "lovely"—and I'm afraid she is not over "young"—but she has one thing in her favour, she has *money*—which, after all, is the real object in this instance.

JACK. All right, dad, as long as you are satisfied, go in and win!

SIR FRANCIS. And I have to thank you, my boy, for the tip.

JACK. Thank *me* for the tip? I don't remember, dad. Who is she? What's her name?

SIR FRANCIS. You'll be delighted when I tell you.

JACK. Yes. Well?

SIR FRANCIS. Can't you guess?

JACK. No, dad, I can't!

SIR FRANCIS. Donna Lucia d'Alvadorez. *(Slapping* JACK *on the shoulder and crossing* L.C.*)*

JACK. What? *(Goes* R.C.—*aside.)* The deuce! *(Turning to* SIR FRANCIS.*)* Dad, this is impossible!

SIR FRANCIS. Impossible? Why, you yourself suggested it, and for your sake, my lad, I'm going to do it.

JACK. But, dad—you can't!

SIR FRANCIS *(with a look off* L.). Can't? Why not? *(Gravely; moving a little nearer to* JACK, C.) Is there anything against the lady's reputation?

JACK. No, but—you *mustn't*—you *can't!*

SIR FRANCIS. "Mustn't," "Can't,"! Why, Jack, what a boy you are! Didn't you tell me to go to the hotel—change my things put a flower in my buttonhole—*(lifting lapel of coat to indicate carnation)* and, by George, Jack, I believe the flower's done the trick!

JACK. She gave it away, dad.

SIR FRANCIS. My dear boy, *(slight nudge)* she's explained all that. *(Goes upstage* L.C. *and returns downstage very self-satisfied.)*

JACK *(aside)*. This is horrible! *(Aloud.)* But, dad, circumstances have altered since then.

SIR FRANCIS *(coming* C.). In what way?

JACK. You know you're too good—you're not the man to be thrown away like this.

SIR FRANCIS *(hand on* JACK'S *shoulder)*. Say no more, my boy—your consideration for me settles it. *(Crosses* R.) It will put you forward years. Had she been young and lovely, she wouldn't have looked at me. As it is, I flatter myself she's taken rather a fancy to me, and as for old Spettigue, in spite of his marked attentions, I don't think he has the ghost of a chance with me. *(Goes up* R.C.)

JACK *(aside in horror, going down* L.C.). Old Spettigue—attentions— Great Heavens, what are we doing? *(Turning, aloud.)* Dad!

SIR FRANCIS *(by arch)*. So wish me luck, Jack, wish me luck.

JACK. Take time, dad, think it over.

SIR FRANCIS *(heroically)*. "Think it over!" That's not the way an old soldier makes love. *(Briskly.)* I'm going into your rooms to get myself a rattling good spanking brandy and soda to bring me up to the mark!

(Exit SIR FRANCIS *to rooms.)*

JACK *(crossing* R.*)*. Great Scot—what's the young monkey doing?

(Enter CHARLEY, L.I.E., *quickly.)*

CHARLEY *(crossing to* JACK, R.C.*)*. Jack! Jack! I wish you'd speak to Babbs—he's carrying on disgracefully. He's taken Amy away from me, and gone off round the garden with her.

JACK. Well, that's nothing to what's going on here.

(Cork pops loudly off in rooms—both turn. CHARLEY *listens, surprised.)*

Hear that?

CHARLEY. Yes, what is it?

JACK. My dad getting himself a "rattling good spanking brandy and soda."

CHARLEY. Brandy and soda? What for?

JACK. To propose to Babbs; that's all! *(Goes down* R.*)*

CHARLEY *(goes* C.*)*. I knew something awful would come of this. We shall be found out and disgraced. How could you let it go on?

JACK *(coming* C.*)*. Well, don't blame *me*—it was the fault of your muddle-headed aunt not knowing her own mind, and leaving us in the lurch. *(Crossing* L.*)* I could strangle her.

CHARLEY *(following* JACK L., *helplessly)*. What shall we do?

JACK. We must find Babbs, and put him up to the governor's game.

CHARLEY *(dazed)*. "Find Babbs"—but, Jack—

JACK. Come on, we can go round the garden different ways until we've got him. *(Pushing* CHARLEY *across.)*

CHARLEY *(turning to* JACK*)*. But, Jack, can't you end this horrible—

JACK. Oh, shut up, we must keep our heads now,

or we'll ruin everything. Come on. *(Pushes* CHARLEY *off* L.)

(Exits after CHARLEY, L. *Re-enter* SIR FRANCIS *from rooms, wiping moustache after his drink.)*

SIR FRANCIS *(coming down* R.C.*).* Now I'm ready for anybody or anything. *(Looks at watch.)* Why doesn't she come? *(Crossing,* L.C.*)* I didn't tell the dear boy—more particularly when he raised objections—but she promised to meet me here in ten minutes—and time's up—time's up. *(Looking off* L.*)*

(Enter SPETTIGUE *through arch up* R.C., *comes down looking off* R., *does not see* SIR FRANCIS.*)*

(Hears step—raising hat, turning C.*)* Ah, my dear Don—

(Raising their hats, they meet C. *and turn away abruptly.)*

SIR FRANCIS *(aside).* That old fool Spettigue! And with my flower in his coat! *(To* SPETTIGUE.*)* Are you —er—looking for anybody?
SPETTIGUE. No. *(Looks off* R.*)*
SIR FRANCIS *(aside).* What's he hanging about here for? *(Aloud, struggling to be civil.)* Are you in want of anything? *(Lights cigarette out of box on table* C. *Sits.)*
SPETTIGUE *(*R.*).* No. I was only thinking it was a very lovely afternoon. Perhaps you haven't seen the garden? It's looking very beautiful. You ought to give it a good look before you go.
SIR FRANCIS. I *will (blowing smoke)* —before I go.

*(*SPETTIGUE *looks off* R. *again.)*

(Aside.) What is he stopping here for? *(Aloud.)* Have a cigarette?

SPETTIGUE. No, thank you, I never smoke in the day time. *(Aside.)* Why does he remain? *(Looking at his watch.)* She promised to meet me here in ten minutes, and time's up, time's up. *(Going up to arch R.C.)*

SIR FRANCIS *(aside)*. What's he stopping for? I must *tell* him to go.

SPETTIGUE *(aside)*. I wish I could think of something to get rid of him.

SIR FRANCIS *(aloud, rising, strolls R.)*. Well—as you are not smoking—

SPETTIGUE. Oh, don't mind me *(crossing behind table to L.U.E., unconcernedly)* don't mind me!

SIR FRANCIS *(turning to SPETTIGUE)*. I was only thinking perhaps it would be as well if you rejoined the ladies in the garden. They might think it rude, both of us being away— *(Sits R. of table, holding up his cigarette.)*

SPETTIGUE *(coming down L.)*. Perhaps so, perhaps so. *(Aside, at L.I.E.)* She's in the garden.

(Exit L.I.E.)

SIR FRANCIS *(rising)*. Well, she doesn't appear to be coming. I think I'll go and have another— *(Going up R.C.)*

(Enter JACK, L.I.E.)

JACK. I say, dad, you haven't seen Donna Lucia, have you?

SIR FRANCIS *(coming down R.C.)*. No, Jack, I've not.

JACK *(aside)*. That's fortunate.

SIR FRANCIS. I'm waiting for her here.

JACK. Waiting for her—here?

SIR FRANCIS. Yes, I've an appointment with her. I didn't tell you before, Jack, but she's due—in fact, she's over-due! So get out, my boy, get out! *(Looks off R.)*

JACK *(aside).* They mustn't meet till I've seen him. *(Aloud.)* Now I come to think of it, dad, I saw her only a moment ago.

SIR FRANCIS. Oh—where? *(Coming* C.*)*

JACK *(pointing off* L.I.E.*).* In the garden.

SIR FRANCIS. In the garden? *(Crossing* L., *hurriedly.)* Hang it, I've just sent old Spettigue there!

(Exit SIR FRANCIS, L.I.E.*)*

JACK. I know Babbs isn't *there,* but where on earth has he got to? *(Crossing* R.*)*

(Enter CHARLEY, L.U.E.*)*

(Hearing steps, turns. To CHARLEY.*)* Well, have you found him?

CHARLEY *(coming down* C. *dejectedly, hat on back of head).* No, haven't you?

JACK. No, and I've looked all over the place for him.

CHARLEY. So have I, and the worst of it is he's got Amy with him. It's a shame.

JACK *(gets* C.*).* I'll kill the little monkey when I get hold of him!

CHARLEY *(catching sight of* LORD FANCOURT *and* AMY *off* R.; *swings* JACK *round facing* R.*).* Look at him! Isn't it too bad?

(Enter LORD FANCOURT *and* AMY, *together* R., *arm-in-arm.* AMY *crosses to* L. *of* CHARLEY.*)*

AMY. Ah, Mr. Wykeham, there you are. Did you think you'd lost us?

CHARLEY (C.). Yes, I'm afraid I did. *(Moves with* AMY *to* C.*)*

JACK (R.C., *aside to* LORD FANCOURT). Where have you been with that girl, you fool?

LORD FANCOURT (R.). Nowhere.

JACK. Stop where you are. I've something to tell you.

LORD FANCOURT. Oh, have you? *(Flounces round, kicking out skirt backwards. Goes up to arch R.C.)*

JACK *(aloud)*. Charley, has Miss Spettigue seen the Chapel? *(Aside to CHARLEY, as he passes him across to R.)* Take her away while I tell Babbs. *(Aloud, walking between them to arch, R.)* You must see the Chapel. It's an awfully pretty Chapel.

(Exit AMY, R. LORD FANCOURT comes down L. of JACK by arch, R.)

CHARLEY *(about to exit, turns angrily)*. Jack, I'll punch his head if he does it again.

(LORD FANCOURT comes aggressively to CHARLEY. JACK between. CHARLEY irritated, strikes down at LORD FANCOURT over JACK'S shoulder. LORD FANCOURT tips CHARLEY'S hat off jeeringly with his closed fan. JACK hustles CHARLEY off R.)

JACK *(turning savagely, stalks LORD FANCOURT with long strides and without speaking to L.; LORD FANCOURT, backing before JACK to L.)*. What the deuce do you mean by this game?

LORD FANCOURT (L.). What game?

JACK (L.C.). You promised to help us.

LORD FANCOURT. Well, I'm doing my best.

JACK. Doing your best? Your business was to look after those two old chaps, and here you are— *(exasperated, turns and strides away R.)* but I've no wish to argue.

LORD FANCOURT *(follows closely in silence, striding in step behind JACK—speaks when R.C.)*. No, I shouldn't argue if I were you.

JACK (R.). Listen. I want to put you on your guard.

LORD FANCOURT. On my guard! Oh, thank you!

JACK. Yes. My dad's going to propose to you.

LORD FANCOURT (*crosses to* C.). Oh, is he? That's all right. (*Stops suddenly* C.) Well, I'm not going to marry him for you or anybody else. I'll see you hanged first.

JACK (*going to him*). Of course not, you idiot. All you've got to do is to be calm and refuse him.

LORD FANCOURT. *Calm* and refuse him! But a proposal puts anyone in a flutter. *You* know that.

JACK. All you've got to do is to remember that you're a real old lady.

LORD FANCOURT. How the dickens am I to remember that I'm a real old lady (*lifts skirt and petticoat together, showing trousers to knees*) —with my trousers on?

JACK (*pulling down* LORD FANCOURT'S *skirt*). Never mind your trousers! (*Looking off* L.I.E.) Look out— here's the dad! I'm off! (*Going up to arch,* R.C.)

LORD FANCOURT (*following up after* JACK, R.C., *and grabbing him*). Yes, but what am I to say? (*Looking toward* L.I.E., *anxiously.*) I've never been proposed to before.

JACK (*in archway*). Oh—say he's taken you by surprise—but, whatever you do, mind you refuse him.

LORD FANCOURT. Oh yes, I'll refuse him.

(*Exit* JACK *through arch to* R. LORD FANCOURT *hides between arch and door to rooms.* SIR FRANCIS *enters,* L.I.E., *looking at watch.*)

SIR FRANCIS. Really, it's too bad. (*Crosses* R., *looks off.*) She made the proposition herself (*crossing upstage to* L.U.E.) —it was a definite proposition of her own—well, (*coming down* L.) ladies are proverbially unpunctual, but—

(LORD FANCOURT, *peeping round corner, appears in archway* R.C., *holding up finger with fichu archly to* SIR FRANCIS.)

LORD FANCOURT. Oo! Oo!

(SIR FRANCIS turns, sees LORD FANCOURT, raises hat. LORD FANCOURT looks coyly at SIR FRANCIS and swings end of fichu gaily round and round.)

SIR FRANCIS *(putting on hat again).* Ah, dear Donna Lucia, here you are! I was beginning to be afraid *(crossing R.)* —and popped into the garden to find you.

(LORD FANCOURT, with long strides, steals quickly across to L.U.E., and is nearly off as SIR FRANCIS says:)

It's so good of you to come. *(Turns.)*

(LORD FANCOURT, seeing SIR FRANCIS turn, stops L.U.E., his attempt to bolt is frustrated.)

(Sees LORD FANCOURT at L.U.E.) Won't you sit down?

(LORD FANCOURT sits L. of C. table.)

(Aside.) By jove, got her at last! Now for the plunge! I'll begin with a compliment. *(Looks at LORD FANCOURT, then away again.)* I wonder what's her real age? However, a woman's never too old for a compliment, so here goes! *(Coming to table—clears throat.)*

(LORD FANCOURT clears throat too.)

(Aloud.) Donna Lucia, you'll pardon the rude metaphor of an old campaigner, I'm sure, but to meet you to-day for the first time, as I have done, is to me like a lonely traveller coming across some—er—bright little floweret— *(Their eyes meet. Indicating L.)* by the wayside.

LORD FANCOURT (*looks* L., *then to* SIR FRANCIS). Do you mean me?

SIR FRANCIS. Yes, Donna Lucia, yes! (*Goes down* R., *aside.*) By George, that's a good start.

LORD FANCOURT (*aside*). What am I to say to that, I wonder? (*Aloud.*) Oh, yes, I think that's very nice and very kind of you.

SIR FRANCIS (*turns away* R., *aside*). By George, she looks anything between fifty and a hundred—!

(JACK *appears in arch at back,* R.C., *shakes fist at* LORD FANCOURT, *who cocks a snook at him, unseen by* SIR FRANCIS. *As* SIR FRANCIS *turns,* LORD FANCOURT *converts "snook" into stroking front hair, looking innocently at* SIR FRANCIS. JACK *retires* R., *unseen by* SIR FRANCIS.)

SIR FRANCIS (*aside*). Well, I've put myself to it, so I must come to the point. (*Clears throat again.*)

LORD FANCOURT. What, again?

SIR FRANCIS (*going to* R. *of table—aloud bluffly*). Donna Lucia, do you know what a man longs for when he's lonely—desolate—and wretched?

LORD FANCOURT. A drink?

SIR FRANCIS (*goes down* R.—*aside*). What a woman —doesn't help one a bit! (*Up to* R. *of table—aloud.*) No, Donna Lucia, this is what he longs for—he longs to plant in his own heart that bright little floweret.

LORD FANCOURT. I know—by the wayside (*pointing* L.) —that one. Does he really?

SIR FRANCIS (*heartily*). Yes, Donna Lucia, yes. (*With lover-like intention.*) And I have come all the way from India to find that little floweret.

LORD FANCOURT. You must be tired. (*Indicating chair.*) Take a chair.

SIR FRANCIS. Thank you. (*Sits* R. *of table* C., *puts hat, crown downwards on* C. *table.*) It's a long way, Donna Lucia.

LORD FANCOURT. Oh, quite a long walk.

SIR FRANCIS. But I have *found* it.

LORD FANCOURT. Then why don't you wear it in your buttonhole? *(Pointing.)*

SIR FRANCIS. Ah, will you let me or will it be given away to another as you did before?

LORD FANCOURT. Ah, yes—I remember, I was a naughty girl this morning. *(Putting corner of fichu in mouth, shaking it to and fro coyly—and putting R. hand unconsciously on table.)*

SIR FRANCIS *(looking away, cautiously).* But, dear Lucia— *(Places hand on that of* LORD FANCOURT'S *for a second and giving it a pat—then removes it and looks off R. again.)*

LORD FANCOURT *(taking hand off table, aside).* He's getting on!

SIR FRANCIS. The floweret I mean must sit at the head of my table—walk by my side—dwell in my heart for ever. *(Places R. hand on heart and with L. hand slightly moves hat. Looks away R.)*

LORD FANCOURT *(rising and looking quickly into hat, sits again; aside).* He's going to show me a conjuring trick.

SIR FRANCIS *(bluffly again).* But I'll waste no more words—I'll come to the point with a soldier's bluntness. Will you be my wife?

(Quick gasp from LORD FANCOURT.*)*

Will you be my little floweret?

LORD FANCOURT. Well, you see— *(then remembering* JACK'S *words)* "you've taken me so much by surprise."

SIR FRANCIS. Then I may hope?

LORD FANCOURT. I'm afraid not. No, don't hope—I wouldn't hope if I were you.

SIR FRANCIS. I beg pardon, Donna Lucia. Do I understand— *(Rises.)*

LORD FANCOURT. I must refuse you. The fact is, I am another's.

SIR FRANCIS. Another's? *(Turns away R.)*

LORD FANCOURT. I say, don't be downhearted—I'll tell you what I'll do if you like.

SIR FRANCIS *(turning eagerly).* Yes, yes.

LORD FANCOURT. I will be a sister to you.

SIR FRANCIS. A sister—only a sister?

LORD FANCOURT. Only a sister. Nothing more.

SIR FRANCIS. And no words of mine can alter your decision?

LORD FANCOURT. I'm afraid not. You see, I'm in a more peculiar position than I could ever explain. I am a woman with a history.

SIR FRANCIS. Then it is quite useless our prolonging this interview. *(Goes to back of table.)* And you will accept my regrets and *(picks up hat and goes down L.)* —apologies for ever having broached the subject?

LORD FANCOURT. Oh, certainly! Any time you're passing—

SIR FRANCIS *(puts on hat—aside).* Refused. What a relief! I'm sorry, though, for the boy's sake.

(SIR FRANCIS *exits*, L.I.E. *Enter* JACK *up* R.C., *from* R.)

LORD FANCOURT *(rising).* Well, here's a nice position!

JACK *(meeting* LORD FANCOURT, C.). You fool, what did you want to make a fool of my dad like that for?

LORD FANCOURT *(rapidly).* I didn't make a fool of the fool, you fool! Did you hear what he called me?

JACK. Yes, a floweret.

LORD FANCOURT. Yes—by the wayside—that's a nice thing, isn't it?

JACK. Why didn't you cut him short, and refuse him at once?

LORD FANCOURT. I couldn't refuse him until he'd proposed—no lady could. Why, I shall find myself in the divorce court before I know where I am. *(Looks off,*

L.I.E. *Sees* SPETTIGUE; *crossing quickly in front of* JACK.) Look out, here's old Spettigue. *(Turning to* JACK *again, pulls up sleeve which shows shirt cuff, shaking fist.)* I shall land him one—I know I shall— I'm off!

(Takes up skirts and runs off quickly through archway down R. JACK *in front of* C. *table. Enter* SPETTIGUE, L.I.E.)*

SPETTIGUE *(to* JACK *as he enters).* Ah, Mr. Chesney—have you seen—? *(Sees* LORD FANCOURT *off through archway down* R.) Ah!

(Absently pushes JACK, *who sits suddenly on table* C. SPETTIGUE *exits hurriedly by archway* R.)*

JACK. What the deuce did he bolt like that for? Anyhow, they don't wreck my future happiness. *(Rising, looks off* R.) I must find Kitty. Why couldn't Charley's aunt behave like a lady and turn up as she promised *(going* L.) —instead of giving us all this trouble. I hate the sight of her before I've even seen her.

(Exit L.I.E. *A pause.)*

DONNA LUCIA *(off).* First door to the left? Thank you very much.

(Enter DONNA LUCIA, *with opened sunshade framing her head, and* ELA, *by archway* R.C., *from* R.
DONNA LUCIA *is a well-preserved beautiful, kindly woman of middle age, with a young face, but grey hair. She has a keen sense of humour, and is capable of taking command of any situation. On no account sentimental, but with a deep feeling of real sentiment in her nature. This part should be played gaily with a light firm touch of comedy, amusement dominating her performance, and she dominating the situations*

*from now on. Wears afternoon summer dress and
coat to match, hat and gloves, and carries several
visiting-cards in her purse-bag.*

ELA DELAHAY *is a young, pretty, unaffected little
girl of seventeen or twenty. Also has a sense of humour and high spirits. This part should not be played
either sloppily or sentimentally. Wears summer dress
and hat and carries purse-bag and gloves.)*

DONNA LUCIA *(looks round, then crosses behind
table to* L.U.E.). The first door to the left, the man said,
Ela.

ELA *(at door up* R.C.). Yes, here it is. *(Reads on
door.)* "Mr. John Chesney." *(To* DONNA LUCIA.)
Shall I knock?

DONNA LUCIA. Yes, do, my dear.

(ELA *knocks.)*

(Coming down L.C. *Thoughtfully.)* "Chesney." The
name sounds familiar. *(To* ELA.) Why couldn't my
nephew remain in his rooms, and not compel me to
follow him about like this.

ELA *(coming* R.C.). You telegraphed to say you
couldn't come.

DONNA LUCIA *(smiling).* I know, my dear.

ELA. And then you changed your mind.

DONNA LUCIA *(moving to* L. *of table).* Yes—for
about the first time in my life.

ELA. Why?

DONNA LUCIA. Some vague desire to see him without
his knowing. Knock again, dear. *(Closes sunshade.)*

(ELA *knocks.)*

ELA *(coming down* R.). The porter said they might
all be in the garden. *(With childlike enthusiasm.)* I
could roam about these old places all day. Isn't it all
beautiful? *(Looking about excitedly.)*

DONNA LUCIA. Dream away, Ela—I shall wait till someone comes. *(Sits L. of table.)*

ELA *(R.C.; looking round: thrilled, quickly).* Oh, to live among these leafy shades, ancient spires and sculptured nooks—like silent music, a scholar's fairyland!

DONNA LUCIA *(with quiet humour).* But to one poor sublunary being—not quite so young as she used to be—a little fatiguing.

ELA *(behind R. chair of C. table—impetuously to* DONNA LUCIA*).* And how lovely it must be by moonlight, where the shadows have no sudden fears, but are only folds in the mantle of sleep, and all is peace! And the silver bells chime to the sentinel angel of the night, who smiles to Heaven and whispers back, "All's well, sweet bells, all's well!"

DONNA LUCIA. You fanciful little woman. But what has put all this about angels and so forth into your head to-day?

ELA *(going behind table to C., absently).* Oh, I don't know.

DONNA LUCIA *(teasingly).* I think I can trace back all the little by-ways and sly ways of thought that generally lead in *one* direction.

ELA *(going quickly to L. of* DONNA LUCIA *and kneels).* Oh, no, it's all so sweet here—

DONNA LUCIA *(mischievously).* So it was there—"by moonlight," seen from the bridge of a certain yacht— "the rippling sea, the blue night, and brilliant stars"— you see how I remember your words—and a certain "someone" who told you, as you listened to the chime of the ship's bell, that you looked like "the angel of the watch"— He was a flattering-tongued person, that "someone," what was his name again?

ELA *(looking down shyly).* I've told you so often.

DONNA LUCIA *(looking straight ahead, with a smile).* "Lord Fancourt Babberley." *(Fraction of a pause. To* ELA.*)* But I don't want your mind fixed on these things, my dear. *(Changing tone.)* Why, I'd almost forgotten to tell you. I've invested your poor father's money for

you, and thanks to his forethought for his little girl—
he has rendered you independent for life, and what is
worse, independent of me.

ELA *(thoughtfully).* Independent!

DONNA LUCIA. But you won't be, Ela?

ELA *(affectionately).* No.

DONNA LUCIA. For I've grown to love the little orphan I met in such grief in a strange land so much,
that I am not independent of *her.* So let's make a bar-
gain. Put that dreadful evidence of my dependence
aside, and let it grow, and be my little girl and call me
"Auntie," will you?

ELA *(rising and kissing* DONNA LUCIA). Yes, Auntie,
yes. *(Going behind chair* R.C.)

DONNA LUCIA *(slight pause).* How did your poor
father come to have so large a sum of money by him
like that? I thought he'd lost it all.

ELA *(diffidently).* Papa won it at cards.

DONNA LUCIA. Won it at cards? When?

ELA *(looking down).* During his illness.

DONNA LUCIA. From whom?

ELA *(reluctantly).* From Lord Fancourt Babberley.

DONNA LUCIA. Is Lord Babberley a gambler, too?

ELA. *No!*

DONNA LUCIA *(seeing the position and smiling to
herself).* Oh! *(Slight pause.)*

ELA *(eagerly).* But, auntie, if ever we meet, may I
give it back?

DONNA LUCIA. I don't think he'd take it.

ELA. Why not?

DONNA LUCIA. It seems to me he took too much
trouble to lose it! *(Changing tone.)* But *I'm* not going
to speak for him. I don't want you ever to leave me.
(Pause.) Ah, my dear, *(laughing quietly)* you've set
me thinking now.

ELA. Have I, what about?

(ELA *crosses back to* L. *of* DONNA LUCIA.)

DONNA LUCIA. Oh, all about—"someone"—who—
ELA. Oh! Do tell me. *(Kneels.)*

DONNA LUCIA. It was before I went abroad—to Brazil—I was very young and he was very shy. He never called me "the angel of the watch," but he did get as far as a stammering compliment and a blush—and then—

ELA. And then—?

DONNA LUCIA *(with a mock heroic wave of the hand)*. Then he was ordered off with his regiment.

ELA *(with slight diffidence)*. *Without—ever—?*

DONNA LUCIA. Without—*ever! (With finality.)*

ELA *(regretfully)*. Oh—Auntie! *(Sits back on heels, looking up at* DONNA LUCIA.)

DONNA LUCIA *(tiny pause—softly, reminiscently, with slight touch of sentiment almost like a young girl)*. It was at a dance the evening before he went away.

(ELA keeps same tone as DONNA LUCIA *so as not to break her memory.)*

ELA. And you've never loved anyone *since!*

DONNA LUCIA *(smiling quietly)*. I was a sentimental young lady in those days.

ELA. What was his name, auntie?

DONNA LUCIA. Frank Chesney— *(Rises, recollecting—with quick glance towards door.)* How strange!

(ELA rises up R.C. *Enter* SIR FRANCIS, L.I.E.)

(Turning to SIR FRANCIS.) I'm afraid we're intruding.

SIR FRANCIS. Not at all. *(Raising his hat and crossing with slight bow,* R.F.) The college grounds are open to everyone. *(Crosses* R.) I am, so to speak, at home here, merely because these are my son's rooms. *(Turns to* DONNA LUCIA, *indicating rooms with a step towards* R.C.)

DONNA LUCIA. Mr.—?

SIR FRANCIS *(stopping down* R.*)*. Chesney.

(ELA *goes quietly up* L., *turns and watches scene.)*

DONNA LUCIA (C.). And you—pardon my asking— are you—or rather, *were* you—Lieutenant Frank Chesney?

SIR FRANCIS *(interested)*. I was.

DONNA LUCIA. And you don't remember me?

SIR FRANCIS. I acknowledge with regret that I have— er—no recollection whatever— *(But sounding as though he wished he had.)*

DONNA LUCIA. It must be more than twenty years since— *(Turning to* ELA, *who has come down* L.C.*)*

SIR FRANCIS *(a little let down by the time, and trying to recall)*. Twenty years!

DONNA LUCIA *(aside to* ELA *with mock concern)*. He doesn't remember me! *(Taking out several cards from card-case and looking them through.)*

ELA. Twenty years is a long time, auntie.

SIR FRANCIS *(facing audience down* R., *aside)*. Twenty years! Where was the regiment then—I wonder?

DONNA LUCIA *(reads card)*. "Mrs. Beverley-Smythe"— *(Aside to* ELA.*)* Everyone's card but my own of course. *(Puts it under case. To* SIR FRANCIS.*)* Then you've forgotten the day you first embarked for India?

SIR FRANCIS. No.

DONNA LUCIA. But you've forgotten—the evening before?

SIR FRANCIS *(with a smile of recollection)*. No—not altogether.

DONNA LUCIA *(holding out hand)*. Then—?

SIR FRANCIS *(slowly surprised and delighted)*. Lucy! *(Takes off hat with* L. *hand, going to* DONNA LUCIA *and taking her hand.)* Good gracious!

(ELA *goes up* L., *turns and watches scene sympathetically.)*

(Growing quietly excited.) And to think that at that very dance—but you don't remember *that* of course. *(Lets go her hand, puts on hat again.)*

DONNA LUCIA. No?

SIR FRANCIS. No, because you never knew—but that night, by George, I nearly made you an avowal that— Ah! *(Looking at her admiringly.)* And we've never met in all that time! ! Nearly— *(Sees her pretended dismay.)* Well—over twenty years, we'll say, eh?

DONNA LUCIA *(smiling)*. I'm afraid so.

(ELA *comes down* L.C.)

SIR FRANCIS. I remember the dance perfectly, you were in white—tied up with blue.

DONNA LUCIA *(laughing to* ELA). Tied with blue! Like a chocolate box!

SIR FRANCIS *(with enthusiasm)*. You must see my son, he's a splendid fellow! *(Turning and going a little upstage.)* These are his rooms, or rather, he has lent them to a college friend, a young fellow named Wykeham. *(Returning* R.C.)

DONNA LUCIA *(interested)*. Yes. Wykeham?

SIR FRANCIS. Who is entertaining some ladies—two young ladies (DONNA LUCIA *smiles at* ELA.) —and his aunt.

DONNA LUCIA *(puzzled; turns to* SIR FRANCIS). His aunt.

SIR FRANCIS. A lady from Brazil.

DONNA LUCIA *(astonished—looks front)*. From Brazil!

SIR FRANCIS. Yes. Donna Lucia d'Alvadorez. I must introduce you. *(Goes up* R. *a step or two.)*

ELA *(quickly, aside to her)*. Auntie, what does he mean?

(SIR FRANCIS *returns down* R.)

DONNA LUCIA *(aside, to* ELA*)*. Wait a minute, my
dear. *(Turning to* SIR FRANCIS.*)* Do I understand you
to say that Donna Lucia d'Alvadorez is here, actually
here?

SIR FRANCIS. In the garden *(with look off* R.*)* —or
was five minutes ago. Do you know her?

DONNA LUCIA. I—I've heard of her. *(Turning* C.
Aside, half to ELA *and half to herself.)* Shall I stay and
see this out or return to town and— *(Absently finger-
ing card.)*

SIR FRANCIS. May I trouble you? *(Holding out hand
for card.)*

DONNA LUCIA *(with quick look at* SIR FRANCIS—
gives wrong card). Certainly.

SIR FRANCIS *(reading)*. "Mrs. Beverley-Smythe."
(Crossing behind table to L.I.E.*)*

ELA *(going to* DONNA LUCIA*)*. Auntie!

DONNA LUCIA. Ssh!

SIR FRANCIS *(down* L.*)*. I'll find Donna Lucia, and
the boys, or perhaps you wouldn't mind coming into
the garden to them?

DONNA LUCIA *(picking up sunshade by table. Crossing* ELA *to* C.*)*. With pleasure. I'm quite curious to
see them. *(To* SIR FRANCIS, *introducing.)* My niece,
Miss Delahay.

SIR FRANCIS. How do you do?

DONNA LUCIA. Er—Colonel?

SIR FRANCIS *(with slight bow)*. Sir Francis Chesney.
(At L.I.E.*)*

DONNA LUCIA. Come, Ela.

(ELA *and* DONNA LUCIA *exeunt* L.I.E.)

SIR FRANCIS *(at* L.I.E., *replaces hat on head, enthusiastically)*. Ah, Jack, my boy, if that had been Donna
Lucia—things might have been very different.

(Exits L.I.E. *after them.* LORD FANCOURT, R.I.E., *runs
rapidly across stage, holding up skirts in front only*

so that SPETTIGUE, *following, does not see trousers, and exits* L.I.E.

Enter SPETTIGUE, R.I.E., *runs across stage, out of breath, top-hat wobbling perilously and exits* L.I.E., *following* LORD FANCOURT.

Enter BRASSETT *from house, stops in archway with tablecloth, sees* LORD FANCOURT *and* SPETTIGUE, *comes down and looks off* L. *after them.)*

BRASSETT. What's his lordship up to with the old gent now? Looks as if they were having a game of some kind. I think it's very dangerous, running about like that. I'm not sure I didn't catch sight of his lordship's trousers. *(Takes cigarette box off* C. *table and puts it on table at back.)*

(Enter JACK *and* KITTY, R.C.)

JACK *(entering* L. *of* KITTY, *talking ardently).* And now here we are at last—no one here, and I can speak to you. Kitty, my dear Kitty—

(BRASSETT, behind C. *table, lays cloth.)*

KITTY *(sees* BRASSETT—*aside to* JACK). But, Jack, look!

(KITTY crosses to L.U.E., *behind* BRASSETT.)

JACK *(turns, sees* BRASSETT, *goes to him* R.C.—*aside).* What are you doing, Brassett?
BRASSETT. Laying the cloth for tea, sir.
JACK. Go away!
BRASSETT. But you gave orders, sir. *(Goes slowly behind* JACK *to* R.)

(KITTY drops down L.C.)

JACK. Put it back for half an hour. Quick, man, can't you see I'm engaged?

(BRASSETT R.C. JACK C., *standing behind table.*)

BRASSETT (*looking from* KITTY *to* JACK). Really, sir? (*Looks at* KITTY—*then to* JACK.) I congratulate you.

(KITTY *turns away* L. *to hide laughter.*)

JACK. Busy, confound you! Get out and don't come back!

(*Quickly puts tea-cloth over* BRASSETT's *head, pushing him off through door to rooms* R. BRASSETT *exits to rooms.* KITTY *goes* L. *of* C. *table and sits.*)

(*Coming behind table* C. *to* KITTY.) And now, my dear Kitty—

KITTY (*amused*). Yes, Jack, you've said that before.

JACK. Now don't interrupt me. I go straight at most things, and I'm not going to hesitate over this.

KITTY. Is it that you attach so much importance to it, or that you don't care what you do?

JACK. It's both—*mixed*—so, Kitty, my dear Kitty—

KITTY (*still chaffingly, looking up at him*). Yes, Jack?

JACK. Ah, Kitty—do be serious. In a few hours you'll be hundreds of miles away, and it may be years before we meet again—unless—unless—

KITTY (*still mischievously*). Unless— (*another upward look at him*) what?

JACK (*swallowing it*). Will you listen?

KITTY (*with mock helplessness*). I can't help myself.

JACK (*sits* R. *of table, seriously*). I've told you how my father intended me for Parliament and all that?

KITTY. Yes.

JACK. Well, he tells me now, that for the next few years I shall have to give up all that, and earn my own living.

KITTY. Well, that will do you no harm, Jack.

JACK *(brightly, much encouraged)*. No, that's how I look at it. I've done well up here, I've worked hard, and work tells wherever you are—so I intend to turn to—and come out all right—one way or another. *(Rising, going down R. Aside.)* I've broken the ice at last! *(Goes up quickly to arch R.C.)*

KITTY *(aside, quickly)*. The dear fellow!

JACK *(aside—looking off to R.)*. I hope they'll keep away.

KITTY *(chaffingly over shoulder to JACK up R.C.)*. I'm sure I wish you every success.

JACK *(coming to back of table)*. Of course—*in time* —I shall be all right, but the question is, will you wait?

KITTY. Wait? *(Looking full at him.)* What for?

JACK *(disconcerted, drawing to R. of chair, R. of table; quickly and nervously)*. No. I beg pardon—I didn't mean that.

KITTY. Oh, you didn't mean it?

JACK *(bravely)*. No. What I *really* mean is, that— before I say anything further—I should like you to understand *(his courage melting)* —what I've been telling you.

KITTY *(after a little pause)*. Oh, yes— *(Cruelly.)* What was that?

JACK *(sits R. of table)*. Well, to be practical and lay everything fairly before you—my position in life will be something in—er—

KITTY. The City.

JACK. Thanks. My home—er—

KITTY. Surburban.

JACK. Thanks. Exactly! Transit—

KITTY. 'Bus or rail.

JACK. My personal income—

KITTY. Small.

JACK. My extra income—

KITTY. Precarious.

JACK. But under certain conditions my fears would be nil—and my hopes *tremendous! !* *(Enthusiastically*

—rising.) Now you know all *(sits)* —that's how I stand.

KITTY *(pointedly, nodding to chair)*. Oh, *that's* how you stand.

JACK *(rising, laughs)*. Oh, Kitty! *(Goes* R., *looks off. Aside, quickly.)* It's my duty to tell her all— *(Going up* R.C. *to arch, looking off* R.*)*

KITTY *(aside, quickly)*. The dear fellow!

JACK *(looking off* R., *shaking fist; aside)*. I'll kill anyone who comes now!

KITTY *(affecting a kindly but unconcerned interest)*. Well, I hope those happy conditions will be realised to your heart's content.

JACK *(coming down to* L. *of* KITTY, *sincerely)*. Kitty, my dear Kitty—they will never be realised—without *you.*

KITTY *(rises, goes a little to* C.*)*. Without me?

JACK *(draws back apologetically; goes down* L.*)*. Now you're vexed with me. You hate the City! ! You despise the suburbs! ! You loathe 'buses! ! !

KITTY *(reprovingly and affectionately, turning, facing* JACK L.*)*. Why should you say that, Jack?

JACK *(turning in wonder)*. Kitty!

KITTY *(in front of* C. *table)*. As if I hadn't the heart to do what thousands of better girls than I have done.

JACK *(a step towards her, surprised)*. Kitty!

KITTY *(sitting on edge of table)*. As if I couldn't guess all the happy fun that is to be got out of cooking and mending—and ministering to the wants and happiness of the man who will work and strive for the woman he loves!

JACK *(hopefully, going a step nearer)*. Then, Kitty—?

KITTY *(rising—holding out hand)*. Try me, Jack, for I love you dearly.

JACK *(taking both her hands)*. You *do*, Kitty, you *do?*

KITTY. As much *(teasing again)* —as much as you love me, Jack.

JACK *(exultantly)*. KITTY! *(Going to kiss her.)*

KITTY *(facing* JACK *laughingly)*. "My dear Kitty—"

JACK. "My *dear* Kitty," you're a brick!

*(*JACK *puts his arms round* KITTY *and kisses her.* KITTY *then runs up* R.C.*—looks off, and* JACK *goes down* L.C.*)*

(Exultantly.) I've done it! *(Facing audience down* L.*)* I've done it! !—in spite of the lot of 'em! ! ! *(Goes up* L. *Walks up and down delightedly.)*

*(*KITTY *turns and seeing* JACK *walking up and down, she laughs.)*

KITTY *(comes down* R.C.*)*. Oh, but what about my guardian, Mr. Spettigue?

*(*JACK, *coming* C., *puts arm round* KITTY*—both sit on table* C.*)*

JACK *(decisively)*. I'll see him at once.

KITTY *(alarmed)*. No, *that* won't do.

JACK. Won't do?

KITTY. No, I must have his consent in *writing*.

JACK. In writing, why?

KITTY. So that he can't retract. *(Crossing* L.*)* You don't know him as well as I do. Now, there's only *one* person who can get that written consent for us, so be a good boy and send her to me at once. *(Crossing* JACK *to* L.I.E.*)*

JACK *(rising)*. What, Amy—?

KITTY *(returning* L.C.*)*. No, Charley's aunt—Donna Lucia.

JACK *(staggered)*. Donna Lucia! But, Kitty—

KITTY. Now, don't ask questions, there's a good **boy,** but send her to me at once while I find Amy.

(Exits L.I.E.*)*

JACK *(crosses* R.*)*. Where are we now? This can't go on. *(Looks off* R.I.E.*)*

(Enter CHARLEY, L.I.E., *running. Bangs* JACK *on back.)*

CHARLEY. I've done it, Jack, I've done it!

JACK. Done what? *(Meeting* CHARLEY R.C.*)*

CHARLEY. I've let the cat out of the bag, and *told* her *everything*.

JACK. You fool! *(Backing* CHARLEY *to* C., *holding him by coat.)* What for—told her what?

CHARLEY *(surprised)*. That I love her.

JACK *(with relief, letting him go)*. Oh, is that all?

CHARLEY *(changing tone)*. Yes, but Jack, she's gone off to find Donna Lucia to get her uncle's consent. We shall be in the dickens of a mess yet.

JACK. Well, keep cool, man, keep cool! We're all right up to now. We're all right up to now! *(Both coming down* R.C., *beyond table.)*

(Enter LORD FANCOURT, L.I.E., *running (no fan this entrance), doubles between boys* R.C. *and hides behind* C. *arch,* L. *side of it. Boys, catching sight of* SPETTIGUE L., *go up* R.C., *trying to look unconcerned. Enter* SPETTIGUE, L.I.E.*)*

SPETTIGUE *(strolls across stage humming, out of tune)*.
    "When and how shall I earliest meet her,
    What are the words she'll first say to me—"

(Exits R.I.E. *Boys watch* SPETTIGUE *off over their shoulders, then cross to arch* L. *and bring* LORD FANCOURT *down—*JACK R., CHARLEY L. *of* LORD FANCOURT.*)*

CHARLEY. You'll drag us into awful disgrace.

LORD FANCOURT *(between them* C.*).* And a dem'd good job, too! You don't know the things he keeps on saying to me.

JACK *(abusively).* He? Who?

LORD FANCOURT. Why, my mash—old Spettigue.

JACK *(impatiently).* Well, what does he say?

CHARLEY. Yes, what does he say?

LORD FANCOURT *(with a look at* CHARLEY*).* No, Charley's too young. *(Pushes* CHARLEY *away, whispers to* JACK.*)*

(CHARLEY, *looking sulky, tries to hear.)*

JACK. Get out, man, that's nothing.

LORD FANCOURT. No, but it's very embarrassing. Look how well I get on with the girls.

JACK. Yes, confound you, too well.

LORD FANCOURT. Oh, do I. *(Kicks skirt out of his way as he turns, goes up and puts brooch on table, back. Then leans against arch* R.I.E., *feet crossed.)*

CHARLEY *(with sudden frenzy).* Jack, I can live this lie no longer. *(Sits* L. *of table* C.*)*

JACK *(shouting aggressively).* Now, don't start that! Some lies have got to be lived.

CHARLEY. What for?

JACK *(savagely).* To save confessing them, you duffer! *(Sits* R. *of table.)*

CHARLEY *(despairingly).* I wish to goodness you'd bring it all to an end.

LORD FANCOURT. So do I! I want a drink!

JACK *(working himself up; to* CHARLEY, *but spoken at* LORD FANCOURT*).* We'd be all right if the donkey would only be reasonable and behave like a lady.

CHARLEY. I know all that, but he can't—he doesn't know how.

JACK. As it is, the selfish idiot's ruining and spoiling everything.

(LORD FANCOURT *listens to this abuse, looking hurt. Takes off fichu and flings it down in silence.*)

CHARLEY. I wish we'd asked Freddy Peel now.
JACK. At any rate, Freddy Peel would have stood by us like a man.

(LORD FANCOURT *undoing dress.*)

CHARLEY. We were fools to trust him.
JACK. The selfish little beast!

(LORD FANCOURT *lets dress slip to the ground and steps over it.*)

CHARLEY. When you think of all the misery he's put us to.

(LORD FANCOURT *takes off petticoat and steps over that, looking injured, with hands in his pockets.*)

JACK. I feel so infernally indignant, I could wring his head off.

(LORD FANCOURT, *down* R., *turns back to audience, stands grinning, hands in trouser pockets, facing boys—defying them. He is now in shirt sleeves, waistcoat and trousers, but still wearing wig, bonnet and mittens.*)

CHARLEY (*seeing* LORD FANCOURT). Look—look at him now!

(LORD FANCOURT *bolts through archway up* R.C., *followed by* JACK, *who picks up petticoat and fichu.* CHARLEY *picks up dress—round back of scene—re-enter* R.I.E. *after a second, followed by* SPETTIGUE. *Exeunt up* R.C. *again. They re-enter down* R.I.E. *still running same order, cross stage to* L.U.E. *Exit* LORD

FANCOURT L.U.E. *as* SPETTIGUE *re-enters* R.I.E. JACK *and* CHARLEY *stop up* L. *They quickly hide dress, etc., behind their backs.)*

SPETTIGUE *(to* JACK, *breathlessly).* Ah, Mr. Ches-ney, have you seen Donna Lucia?

(JACK *and* CHARLEY *point off* L.I.E.)

JACK. In the garden.

(Exit SPETTIGUE L.I.E. JACK *and* CHARLEY L.U.E. *and return dragging* LORD FANCOURT *down* C. CHARLEY R. *of him,* JACK L.)

LORD FANCOURT (C., *throwing them off).* Here, you chaps—I won't stand this any longer, let Charley have a go.

(CHARLEY *goes down* R. JACK *puts fichu half in* L. *coat pocket. gets petticoat ready to put over* LORD FANCOURT'S *head.)*

(LORD FANCOURT *puts his hands in pockets in sulky refusal.* JACK *drops petticoat over* LORD FANCOURT'S *head and tries to fasten it round his waist while standing behind him, finding it won't meet, comes forward to see the cause and makes* LORD FAN-COURT *take his hands out of his pockets.)*

Take your hands out of your pockets.

(LORD FANCOURT *does so and petticoat falls to the ground.* JACK *pulls it up.* LORD FANCOURT *fastens it.)*

Here are your braces.

(JACK *hands* R. *elastic brace to* LORD FANCOURT *who lets it slip, hitting* JACK *in the eye.* JACK *gives brace*

again, LORD FANCOURT *fastens it while* JACK *takes*
L. *brace, turns towards* L.I.E. *looking off anxiously,*
brace springs out of his hand and hits LORD FAN-
COURT. JACK *grins,* LORD FANCOURT *goes down* L.
JACK *crosses* R. *to* CHARLEY, *picks up bottom of dress*
which CHARLEY *is holding by the shoulders with*
sleeves hanging down. LORD FANCOURT *turning,*
sees them holding dress horizontally, runs and dives
into it, then shakes CHARLEY *by the hand as his arm*
comes out of R. *sleeve. When* LORD FANCOURT *gets*
his collar fastened, JACK *speaks.*)

JACK. Just when we want old Spettigue in his best
humour, you go and risk everything by this fool of a
game.

LORD FANCOURT *(doing up dress).* What fool of a
game? I'm not going to marry old Spettigue—I could
never be happy with a man like that.

CHARLEY. You know, Babbs, if it was your little
girl, we'd do anything for you.

LORD FANCOURT. Where's my antimacassar?

JACK *(putting fichu round* LORD FANCOURT). And
all you think of is running after our girls, confound
you.

LORD FANCOURT. Charley, am I all right behind?
(Straightening down his things, turns back to audience
and gives his skirt a final flirt out behind with both
hands.)

(All go up R.C., *as though to exit,* CHARLEY *looks*
L.I.E.)

JACK. Look out—here are the girls!

*(They stop—*LORD FANCOURT *crosses* L. *behind table to*
L.C. *Enter* KITTY *and* AMY, L.I.E.)

KITTY *(going to* L.C. *by table).* Oh, Donna Lucia,
we've been looking for you everywhere. *(Indicating*

chair L. *of table to* JACK, *taking* LORD FANCOURT'S *arm and leading him down* L.C.) Amy and I want so much to speak to you.

AMY *(having taken* LORD FANCOURT'S L. *arm).* We're in a difficulty.

LORD FANCOURT. A difficulty?

(CHARLEY *goes* L. *of* AMY L. JACK *brings chair from* L. *of table and places it behind* LORD FANCOURT, L.C., *then goes to* R. *of* KITTY.)

KITTY. And we want you to be an angel— *(Aside, to* JACK.) Now Jack, do go away!

AMY. Yes, Charley, do go away.

LORD FANCOURT *(to boys).* Go away, they want me to be an angel.

(JACK *and* CHARLEY *go up* L.C. KITTY *kneels* R. *of* LORD FANCOURT; AMY L.)

KITTY *(to* LORD FANCOURT). You know Amy's uncle, Mr. Spettigue, is my guardian, and under my father's will, gets nearly all my money if I marry without his consent.

AMY. And you know Jack and Kitty are in love with each other, and Jack's lost all his money or something—

KITTY *(getting quicker).* For years and years—

(LORD FANCOURT *looks at each in turn.)*

AMY *(and quicker).* And Kitty wants you to—

KITTY. No, wait a moment, Amy dear.

LORD FANCOURT *(to* AMY). Yes, wait a moment, Amy dear. *(Places his arm round* AMY.) It's her turn now.

(JACK *restrains* CHARLEY *from punching* LORD FAN-COURT.)

AMY *(to* KITTY). Now it's your turn.
LORD FANCOURT *(to* KITTY). Yes, now it's your turn.
(Places arm round KITTY.)

(CHARLEY *prevents* JACK *from hitting* LORD FAN-
COURT.)

KITTY. And Amy and Charley are in love with each
other, too. But you don't object, do you? *(Rises.)*
LORD FANCOURT. Oh, no, my dears.

(AMY *rises.*)

KITTY. You old dear! ⎱ *(together; kissing* LORD
AMY. You dear thing! ⎰   FANCOURT).

(They go up together and look off L.U.E. JACK *and*
CHARLEY *come down* R. *and* L. *of* LORD FANCOURT
and punch him. KITTY *and* AMY *return to* R. *and* L.
of LORD FANCOURT.)

KITTY *(to* JACK). Now, Jack, do go away.
AMY *(to* CHARLEY). Yes, go away, Charley.
LORD FANCOURT *(between girls).* Yes, go away. We
three girls want to be alone.

(JACK *and* CHARLEY *go up* L.C. KITTY *kneels* R. AMY
L. *as before.*)

CHARLEY *(aside to* JACK). I must end this—I must
do something!
JACK. Well, go and look after the tea.

(Exit CHARLEY, R.C., *to rooms.)*

I must bring them all and stop this.

(Exit hurriedly L.U.E.)

KITTY *(to* LORD FANCOURT). Now, first—you know where we left off, don't you?

LORD FANCOURT. Yes, you're all in love and want to get married.

KITTY. Well—er—yes.

AMY. And we want uncle's consent.

KITTY. And yours. And we want you to be an angel and do it.

LORD FANCOURT. "An angel and do it?" Do what?

KITTY *(a little anxiously).* Why, get Mr. Spettigue's consent.

AMY. For both of us.

LORD FANCOURT. Oh, for both of you.

KITTY. Yes, first, you see, *you'll* give *your* consent to Charley and Amy, won't you?

LORD FANCOURT *(to* AMY). Oh, yes—nothing could be nicer.

AMY. You *are* so kind—but I knew it from the first.

LORD FANCOURT *(to* AMY). Would you like me to be one of your bridesmaids?

(They look away embarrassed and sit back on their heels.)

No? Some other time.

KITTY. Well, now we want you to get his consent, but mine, being a legal affair—you understand, don't you?

LORD FANCOURT. Oh, yes, your father's will, you mean?

KITTY. Yes, his consent must be in *writing.*

LORD FANCOURT. In writing.

KITTY. And you must get it.

LORD FANCOURT *(blandly).* Get it?

KITTY. Yes—you must make him write a letter or something.

LORD FANCOURT. Oh, but my dears, *I've* no influence over him.

AMY. Oh, but you're so clever and so kind.

KITTY. And so rich.

LORD FANCOURT. Oh, yes, and so rich—I remember I gave away half-a-crown only this morning.

KITTY. At any rate, you must try.

AMY. Oh, dear Donna Lucia, *do* say you will try.

KITTY. We are going away—

LORD FANCOURT. Oh! My darlings, don't leave me. *(Puts his arms round them.)*

AMY. Yes, we're going to Scotland.

LORD FANCOURT. Scotland! I know—a beautiful country—where the whiskey comes from.

(Movement of surprise from girls. LORD FANCOURT takes his arms away.)

KITTY. And you are our only hope.

AMY. Oh, Donna Lucia—have *you* ever been in love?

LORD FANCOURT. Oh, yes, dozens of times.

(Movement of surprise from girls.)

I mean—*once* in love *always* in love, you know.

(KITTY rises.)

AMY. Then you know what it means to us, don't you?

LORD FANCOURT. I should rather think I did.

KITTY. And you'll get his consent for us, won't you?

(AMY rises.)

LORD FANCOURT. Well, I'll do my best.

(KITTY goes c.)

AMY. You can't say "No" now. *(Crosses behind LORD FANCOURT to KITTY c.)*

LORD FANCOURT. No—not now.

KITTY. Then we'll find Mr. Spettigue *(taking* AMY's *arm*—C. *going* R.I.E.) and send him to you at once.

(Exeunt KITTY *and* AMY *quickly* R.I.E.)

LORD FANCOURT *(rising, going* R.). Well, here's a deuce of a mess.

(Enter BRASSETT *from rooms* R.C. *Slight pause as they catch each other's eye and smile.)*

Oh, I say, Brassett—can you get me a brandy and soda? No. Here's old Spettigue coming!

*(*BRASSETT *crosses above table and replaces chair beside* L. *table, from down* L., *taking cushions from chair and placing them in chair at back. Exits into rooms* R.C. *Enter* SPETTIGUE, L.I.E., *wearing property top-hat with tin lining.)*

SPETTIGUE *(places hat—crown down—on chair* L. *of table* C. *To* LORD FANCOURT). Ah, there you are, dear Donna Lucia. *(Behind table.)* I have been looking for you all the afternoon.

(Enter DONNA LUCIA, L.I.E.)

I have so much to say to you.
DONNA LUCIA *(coming* L.C.). Mr. Spettigue—Mr Spettigue—

*(*SPETTIGUE *turns.)*

DONNA LUCIA. Will you introduce me to—
SPETTIGUE *(aside).* How annoying! Why couldn't she have kept away? *(Aloud.)* Oh, certainly! Donna Lucia, Mrs. Buttercup-Smith—Donna Lucia d'Alvadorez. *(Goes up* L.)
LORD FANCOURT. How do you do? *(Comes* C.)

(They shake hands, meeting c.)

I'm Charley's aunt from Brazil where the nuts come from.

DONNA LUCIA *(to* LORD FANCOURT, *smiling).* How do you do? Do you know I'm most interested in meeting you?

LORD FANCOURT. Really?

DONNA LUCIA. I knew your late husband—intimately!

(Enter CHARLEY R.C., *in archway.* SPETTIGUE *goes down* L. LORD FANCOURT *turns to fly, but is met by* CHARLEY *in arch* R.C. DONNA LUCIA *crosses down* R., *smiling wickedly.)*

CHARLEY *(stopping him; aside to* LORD FANCOURT). Whatever's the matter, Babbs?

LORD FANCOURT *(in terror, pointing).* She knew my late husband intimately! *(Dashes across to* L.U.E.)

(Enter JACK L.U.E., *meets* LORD FANCOURT *at* L.U.E.)

JACK *(stopping him—to* LORD FANCOURT). Well, how are you getting on? Everything's all right, isn't it?

LORD FANCOURT No! She knew my late husband intimately!

JACK. The deuce!

(Enter BRASSETT *from rooms with tea, which he puts on table* C., *and goes to chair upstage. Enter* KITTY *and* AMY *from* L. *through arch* R.C., *meet* CHARLEY *there up* R.C.)

JACK *(holding* LORD FANCOURT). Look out, here's tea.

LORD FANCOURT. Well, what of it?

(BRASSETT *puts chair from up* C. *behind table.*)

JACK *(aside to* LORD FANCOURT). You must enter-
tain. *(Tucks* LORD FANCOURT'S *arm in his and leads
him to table—aloud, pleasantly—crossing behind* LORD
FANCOURT.) Now, Donna Lucia, will you pour out
tea?

(KITTY *and* AMY *cross back to* L., *followed by* CHAR-
LEY. *Stand talking.* CHARLEY C., AMY L. *and* KITTY
R. *of him.* JACK *offers chair* R. *of table to* DONNA
LUCIA *and stands* R. *of* LORD FANCOURT C.)

LORD FANCOURT. Oh, certainly.

(DONNA LUCIA *sits* R. *of table.)*

SPETTIGUE *(down* L., *aside).* What a cruel interruption! We were getting on so nicely.
LORD FANCOURT. Do we all take tea?

(LORD FANCOURT *neatly pours tea into first cup* L.—
then into one other. AMY *takes it, goes down* L., *gives
it to* SPETTIGUE—*she rejoins* KITTY *and* CHARLEY
up L.C.)

DONNA LUCIA *(to* LORD FANCOURT). You haven't
been in England long, have you?
JACK *(rapidly, aside to* LORD FANCOURT). Change
the subject.
LORD FANCOURT *(to* DONNA LUCIA). Change the
subject.

(LORD FANCOURT *pours tea into* SPETTIGUE'S *hat on
chair* L. *of table, very neatly, without spilling any,
all of the time talking over his shoulder to* DONNA
LUCIA.)

JACK *(aside to* LORD FANCOURT). No. Do you take
sugar and cream?

LORD FANCOURT *(to* JACK). No. Do you take sugar and cream?

JACK *(aside to* LORD FANCOURT, *losing patience).* Ask *her* if *she* takes sugar and cream. *(Nodding towards* DONNA LUCIA.)

LORD FANCOURT *(to* DONNA LUCIA, *aloud).* Ask her if she takes sugar and cream.

(JACK *catches sight of tea in hat and pulls* LORD FANCOURT'S *sleeve. General consternation from all except* SPETTIGUE, *who does not see tea in hat.* LORD FANCOURT *stops pouring tea into hat and replaces teapot on tray as* SPETTIGUE *says; "I—er—")*

SPETTIGUE. I—er— *(turns, comes* L. *of table, and unconsciously holding cup directly over hat)* I think I should like a little sugar and cream, Donna Lucia.

(LORD FANCOURT *pours cream into cup, then into hat, talking to* SPETTIGUE *meanwhile.)*

(Suddenly discovering tea in hat, puts cup on table and lifts up hat.) My hat, my hat!

(DONNA LUCIA *rises, goes* R.)

LORD FANCOURT *(puts down milk jug, looks apologetically concerned, and takes hat).* I beg your pardon.

(He makes three circular movements with hat to mix the milk and tea, opens lid of teapot, pours tea back into teapot, again without spilling any, hands hat back to SPETTIGUE. SPETTIGUE *takes hat.* LORD FANCOURT *taps bottom of it.* BRASSETT *takes hat from* SPETTIGUE, *who turns away* L., *wiping eye.* LORD FANCOURT *gaily flips down lid of teapot and sits.* BRASSETT *exits to rooms with hat.* SIR FRANCIS *enters* R.I.E., *joins* DONNA LUCIA *down* R.)

SPETTIGUE *(aside)*. I must keep her in the humour. I must see her alone. I have it! They must come to dinner. After dinner, that's the time for my purpose. *(Turning, aloud.)* Pardon me, but I have a little proposition to make.

LORD FANCOURT *(rising)*. Hear, hear!

(JACK *pushes him down again.)*

SPETTIGUE. And I can't take "No."

(Orchestra starts playing very, very softly same melody as in Act I, gradually swells into full volume as the CURTAIN *falls.)*

(Re-enter BRASSETT, R.C. SIR FRANCIS *enters arch* R.I.E., *joins* DONNA LUCIA *down* R.)

BRASSETT *(announcing)*. Mr. Spettigue's carriage.

(Exit BRASSETT, R.C.)

SPETTIGUE. Ah, capital, the very thing. Now I want you—all of you—to come and stay and dine at my house.

AMY. Oh, yes, uncle—how nice of you.

KITTY. That will be delightful.⎤
JACK. Grand idea.   ⎬ *(together).*
CHARLEY. Thanks awfully, sir.   ⎦

SPETTIGUE *(to* LORD FANCOURT*)*. You will return with me in the carriage now, Donna Lucia?

LORD FANCOURT *(rises)*. I can't— it's impossible.

SPETTIGUE. I will take no denial. I want you, all of you, to come.

(Enter ELA, *arch* R.C.)

DONNA LUCIA *(down* R.). I have my niece with me, **Miss Delahay.**

LORD FANCOURT *(looks scared, rises).* Miss Delahay!

*(He must get hold of each side of his dress skirt only,
without catching up petticoat too, preparatory to
throwing skirt over head later.)*

SPETTIGUE. Bring her—delighted!
LORD FANCOURT *(coming C. to* SPETTIGUE, *unconsciously almost shaking his skirts).* No, no. I can't, my
things—my things— *(Turns, meets* ELA C.)

(As LORD FANCOURT *says "No, no, I can't,"* ELA *starts
to speak too.)*

ELA *(looking up at sound of his voice).* That voice—
(Running down to C.) It is—it is! *(Meets* LORD FAN-
COURT C. *as he turns to meet her. Greatly surprised.)*
Oh! *(Turns away disappointed to* DONNA LUCIA.) *No!*

(Music swells to crescendo.)

*(*LORD FANCOURT *puts skirt over his head, falls back
into* SPETTIGUE'S *arms—* SPETTIGUE *catches him.*
JACK *kneels at* LORD FANCOURT'S *feet and holds
down skirt, hiding feet with hat.)*

TABLEAU.

CURTAIN.

ACT THREE

"Dinner lubricates business."—Boswell's Johnson.

SCENE.—*Drawing-room,* SPETTIGUE'S *house.*

Three large French windows opening into garden c. *Large double doors* R. *to open off stage. Fireplace* L. *Door down* L. *below fireplace. Upright piano* L.C., *with screw piano stool (revolving stool). Bookcase and china cabinet* R. *and* L., *small bureau up* R. *Down* R.C., *clover-shaped ottoman with centre pillar (Victorian "redan"). Single chair down* R. *below doors, single chair between each of the sets of French windows.* C. *gas chandelier (or gas brackets on walls.) Oil lamp on the bureau, oil standard lamp by piano. Old-fashioned portraits on walls, flowers in bowls, cushions, etc. Victorian sofa below piano* L., *with cushions. Victorian window curtains and velvet overmantle typically Victorian. Curtain over door down* L. *looped up in Victorian manner.*

The room to be a comfortable sitting-room in a house in North Oxford, but as it is owned by a man of sixty, the furniture is obviously round about 1850.

Lights half down inside scene. Full up when lamp on. Moonlight streams into room C.R. *to* L., *alternate green and blue in batten on cloth outside.*

Orchestra plays first 16 bars of "The Eton Boating Song," as the CURTAIN *starts to rise the next 15 bars are played softly till they fade out.*

BRASSETT *discovered with taper lighting candles. Laughter off* R.

BRASSETT *(listens at door* R.*)*. There they go! Dinner's pretty well over now, and they'll all be in here pretty soon. *(Turning up oil standard lamp up* R.*)* Fancy old Spettigue getting me to come here to-night and butler for him. *(Turning up oil lamp up* L.*)* I suppose he's too mean to have a butler of his own. Well, all I can say is, it's simply marvellous the way his lordship's kept it up! He's played the perfect lady something wonderful!

(Loud laughter and talking off R.*)*

Hullo! What's up now? *(Listens as before.)*

(Voices stop.)

Anyhow, if the worst comes to the worst, I've got his lordship's dress clothes with me. *(Above door* R.*)*

(Enter LORD FANCOURT *quickly* R.*)*

LORD FANCOURT. Brassett, get me a fly, quick; I'm going home. *(Goes up* C.*)*

(Enter CHARLEY *and* JACK *quickly catch* LORD FAN-COURT *and bring him struggling down* C. JACK L. *of him,* CHARLEY R. BRASSETT *exits* R., *closing doors.)*

JACK. You've been going along all right, if you'd only paid more attention to old Spettigue. Why did you bolt from the dinner table like that?

CHARLEY. It's awfully dangerous and unkind of you, you know.

JACK. Instead of behaving in a dignified manner as Charley's aunt, here you are going on like some disgraceful old—old—

LORD FANCOURT. Oh, go on—finish it; *(hands folded as old lady)* "Don't spare me!" *(As a man again.)* You can't say I'm drunk, anyhow—or if I am, it's for the want of it!

JACK. Now look here, Babbs, this game won't do.

CHARLEY. Think of the girls and the solemn promise you gave to help us, for their sakes.

LORD FANCOURT. Yes, but *she* wasn't here then.

JACK. She—who?

LORD FANCOURT. The little girl!

JACK. *What* little girl?

LORD FANCOURT. Miss Delahay.

JACK. What, the girl with Mrs.—What's-her-name-Smythe?

LORD FANCOURT. Yes, Mrs, Butterscotch-Smythe's niece.

(CHARLEY *goes to window* C.)

JACK. Well, what of her?

LORD FANCOURT. Why, she's the little girl I met at Monte Carlo, and this Butterscotch woman is the woman who took her away—and I'm off. *(Bolts up* C.)

JACK. Stop him, Charley—quick!

(CHARLEY *turns, stops him, and brings him down* C.
CHARLEY *goes to door* R.)

You've got us into this deuce of a mess!

LORD FANCOURT. Well, of all the beastly, ungrateful things to say!

JACK. What difference can it make to you now?

LORD FANCOURT. Why, I want to talk to her.

JACK. Talk to her! What about?

LORD FANCOURT. I want to tell her what you fellows have been telling your girls. Hang it! I'm just as much in love as you are.

CHARLEY *(near door* R.). Jack, they'll hear everything.

JACK. Was there ever such an idiot? *(Turns away in disgust.)*

LORD FANCOURT *(loudly)*. No! There never was! Look at me! ! ! I'm a disgrace to my sex! *(Turns and goes up* C.)

JACK. Well, if the worst comes to the worst, we'll take the bull by the horns, and be done with him.

LORD FANCOURT *(turning, coming down* C.; *viciously).* You can take the bull by the tail for all I care, and what's more, you can tell those confounded girls of yours to leave off kissing me before her, *(shouting)* I won't stand it!

JACK *(shouting, to* LORD FANCOURT). Don't shout, you idiot! *(To* CHARLEY.) We'll make some excuse— say she's ill, put him in a fly and be done with him.

LORD FANCOURT *(goes up* R. *to* CHARLEY—*venomously).* And Charley, *you* can make some excuse to Miss Verdun for me.

JACK *(jealously—going to* LORD FANCOURT *up* R.C.). Miss Verdun! What have you got to say to Miss Verdun? Come, out with it!

LORD FANCOURT. Haven't I promised to get old Spettigue's consent in writing, you idiot? You're as helpless as a couple of babies, you want your mothers with you! *(Makes off up* L.C.)

(Voices heard off R.)

BRASSETT *(off* R.). This way, madam.

CHARLEY. They're coming!

JACK *(dragging* LORD FANCOURT *back, pushing him on to ottoman* R.C.). Here, sit down, quick!

(Voices off R. CHARLEY R. *of* LORD FANCOURT; JACK L. *of him.* BRASSETT, *entering doors* R., *showing in ladies. Enter* DONNA LUCIA *and* ELA R., *in full evening dress, carrying long white suede gloves.* DONNA LUCIA *carries a fan,* ELA *smelling salts. All three men rise, but* CHARLEY *pushes* LORD FANCOURT *down again. Exit* BRASSETT, R.)

DONNA LUCIA *(crossing behind ottoman to* C.). How is your aunt, Mr. Wykeham? We were afraid she might be ill.

ELA *(following* DONNA LUCIA *to* R.C. ; *between* JACK *and* DONNA LUCIA). Yes, is there anything the matter?

CHARLEY. Er—auntie's been a little upset by the— by the heat of the dining-room, that's all.

DONNA LUCIA. The heat? I found it rather cold!

JACK. Yes, Charley means that—cold. You see, Donna Lucia's lived so long in a warm climate.

(DONNA LUCIA *turns away to hide her amusement and sits* R. *end of sofa, down* L.)

ELA *(giving* JACK, DONNA LUCIA's *smelling salts).* Won't you try auntie's smelling salts? They're so good.

(LORD FANCOURT *stares studiedly at* ELA.)

JACK. Thank you.

(ELA *crosses behind sofa and sits* L. *of* DONNA LUCIA.)

She's often like this. Isn't she, Charley?

(JACK *shoves smelling salts bottle under* LORD FAN- COURT's *nose.* LORD FANCOURT *sneezes with violence of the smelling salts. Enter* AMY, *followed by* KITTY, R. KITTY *shuts door and joins* AMY C.)

AMY *(coming to* C.). I hope Donna Lucia is all right?

KITTY (R.C.). Yes, is she? *(Between* JACK *and* AMY.)

ELA. Oh, yes, Mr. Chesney says she is all right now.

KITTY *(to* JACK). Well, go and tell Mr. Spettigue, he's most anxious, and leave her with us. *(Takes smell- ing salts from* JACK *and goes up to french windows, placing salts on table* R., *then stands in the moonlight on the terrace.)*

AMY. Yes, we'll look after her now. *(Joins* KITTY *up* C., *on terrace by window* C.)

(Exeunt JACK *and* CHARLEY R., *after shaking fists at* LORD FANCOURT *in a warning manner.)*

LORD FANCOURT *(seeing* JACK *and* CHARLEY *going).* I say, you fellows, don't leave me like this! *(Aside.)* Here's a deuce of a position! *(Looking towards ladies.)* I wonder what they'll talk about? I hope they'll be careful before me!

(Enter BRASSETT R., *with coffee, cream and sugar.)*

ELA *(to* DONNA LUCIA). I wonder who she really is, auntie?

DONNA LUCIA. Oh, some old thing they got after receiving my telegram.

*(*BRASSETT *offers coffee to* DONNA LUCIA, *which she accepts.* ELA *shakes her head in refusal.* BRASSETT *then goes to* KITTY *and* AMY, C. *Each take a cup.)*

ELA *(after* BRASSETT *moves away).* Say something to her, auntie. I like to hear her talk.

DONNA LUCIA. I would, my dear, but *look* at her. If I thought they intended that to be like me, I'd never forgive them.

*(*BRASSETT *crosses to* DONNA LUCIA *and* ELA; *both refuse cream. He goes straight to* KITTY *and* AMY, *up* R. *Loud laughter off* R.)

LORD FANCOURT *(aside).* Hark at the silly fools!

*(*BRASSETT *comes down* R. *of* LORD FANCOURT *with coffee. They look at each other and smile.)*

I say, Brassett, what's the story?

*(*BRASSETT *looks at ladies, sees they are not looking, and whispers to* LORD FANCOURT.)*

Oh, that one! *(Laughs and refuses coffee.)*

(Exit BRASSETT R. *Loud laughter again off* R. KITTY *and* AMY *put coffee cups on table up* R. *and come* C.*)*

DONNA LUCIA *(giving cup to* ELA, *who rises and puts it on piano—sits again).* The gentlemen seem to be enjoying themselves.

KITTY *(putting down cup* R., *comes* C.*).* Yes, they do indeed!

AMY *(going to piano stool* L.C., *sits).* Yes, don't they?

DONNA LUCIA. Do you know, I remember a very funny story—

.   *(*LORD FANCOURT *looks alarmed.)*   .

LORD FANCOURT *(aside in terror).* That's just what I expected—

DONNA LUCIA. —that Dom Pedro was very fond of telling.

LORD FANCOURT *(aside in terror).* I must put a stop to this. *(Aloud.)* Won't one of the young ladies play something, please?

DONNA LUCIA *(to* ELA*).* How rude of her to interrupt like that!

ELA. Oh, she couldn't have heard you, auntie.

KITTY. Oh, do tell us, Mrs. Beverley-Smythe.

AMY. Yes—anything about Dom Pedro would be so interesting—do tell us.

DONNA LUCIA. But perhaps Donna Lucia would prefer to tell Dom Pedro's story herself?

LORD FANCOURT. Tom Pedro?

DONNA LUCIA *(mischievously).* Your late husband, you know, Dom Pedro d'Alvadorez.

LORD FANCOURT. Oh, yes, of course— I know his *name*—but I don't remember his stories. I don't hold with such frivolity. *(Aside.)* It's too bad of those fellows.

ELA *(aside to* DONNA LUCIA). Auntie, don't tease her so, tell the story yourself.

DONNA LUCIA. Well, Dom Pedro, who was the kindest soul in all the world, but *(to* LORD FANCOURT) —will Donna Lucia give me permission?

KITTY *(crossing to* L. *of* LORD FANCOURT). Oh, you won't mind Mrs. Beverley-Smythe telling the story, will you?

AMY *(crossing to* R. *of* LORD FANCOURT). And you'll listen, won't you?

LORD FANCOURT *(resignedly)*. Well, if I must—I must! *(Turning towards* DONNA LUCIA.)

*(*KITTY *arranges cushions for him.)*

DONNA LUCIA. Well, as I said before—Dom Pedro, who was the kindest soul in all the world—once found one of his cellarmen—

*(*LORD FANCOURT *looks uneasy.)*

—tipsy—very tipsy.

LORD FANCOURT. Tut, tut!

DONNA LUCIA. So Dom Pedro, whom the man did not recognise—

LORD FANCOURT. Why, was Dom Pedro tipsy?

KITTY. No, no, the man, Donna Lucia.⎫
AMY. The man was tipsy. ⎬ *(together)*.
⎭

DONNA LUCIA. Dom Pedro was, of course, most abstemious—that is what makes the point of the story.

LORD FANCOURT. Oh, does it?

DONNA LUCIA. So Dom Pedro said to the man, "What would Dom Pedro say if he saw you like this"?

LORD FANCOURT. "Tipsy"—like this?

KITTY. Yes, yes!⎫
AMY. Yes. ⎬ *(together)*.
⎭

LORD FANCOURT. And what did the man say?

DONNA LUCIA. The man said—and that's where it's so funny—

LORD FANCOURT. Oh, is that where we laugh?

KITTY *and* AMY. No, no! *(Together.)*

DONNA LUCIA. The man said, "Oh, that's all right, Dom Pedro's *often like this*."

LORD FANCOURT *(blankly)*. Tipsy?

DONNA LUCIA. Yes.

(General laughter, except LORD FANCOURT. AMY *and* KITTY *go up* C.*)*

LORD FANCOURT *(aside, surprised)*. Well, of all the demned silly stories! *(Suddenly collapses with laughter. To* DONNA LUCIA.*)* What was the man's name?

DONNA LUCIA. Really, I don't know the man's name.

LORD FANCOURT. Oh, that's a pity.

DONNA LUCIA *(getting her own back)*. But don't you remember the story? It was a favourite one of Dom Pedro's.

LORD FANCOURT. Oh, perfectly! I shrieked when I heard it first. *(Forgetting himself, pulling up knees of trousers through his skirt.)* I say, that reminds me of a very funny story. I—

*(*KITTY *and* AMY *come down* L. *of* LORD FANCOURT. *They must not see trouser business: both turn to* LORD FANCOURT *on the words "funny story.")*

(Sees girls, recollecting himself.) Won't one of the young ladies play something, please?

KITTY (C.). Oh, I'm so out of practice. You sing something, Amy!

AMY *(between* LORD FANCOURT *and* KITTY*)*. Oh, I can't—I know nothing new.

LORD FANCOURT. Sing that charming little ballad—*Ta-Ra-Ra-Boomdeay.*

AMY. I'm afraid I can't, Donna Lucia.

DONNA LUCIA *(to* LORD FANCOURT*)*. Won't you sing something for us, Donna Lucia?

LORD FANCOURT. Me?

DONNA LUCIA. Yes, one of those charming little Brazilian songs I've heard Dom Pedro was so fond of.

LORD FANCOURT. Oh, no—I haven't sung since I had the measles.

(KITTY turns upstage to hide laughter. AMY joins her.)

DONNA LUCIA *(aside to ELA)*. What?

LORD FANCOURT. Over forty years ago.

DONNA LUCIA *(aside to ELA)*. Another libel! I was the merest infant.

LORD FANCOURT. But I play a little.

(KITTY gets music stool ready for LORD FANCOURT to sit on and remains standing above piano. AMY goes R.C.)

(Rising—aside.) That's a good idea! I shan't have to talk, and I can drown their conversation! *(Crossing towards piano C.)*

DONNA LUCIA *(to LORD FANCOURT as he is crossing C.)*. I hope you've quite recovered from the shock my niece gave you to-day?

LORD FANCOURT. Oh, yes, I was a little upset, wasn't I? I suffer so much from giddiness. Were you ever giddy?

DONNA LUCIA *(mock indignantly)*. Never!

LORD FANCOURT. I was. *(Going up to piano.)* What shall I play? A little Beethoven or Blue Bells of Scotland?

(LORD FANCOURT plays five-finger exercise C to G and back, then quickly strikes B twice, two octaves higher.)

Do you know that? *(Then starts to play something softly.)*

(After a bar or two of music.)

SPETTIGUE (off R.). Come along, my dear friends, come along!

KITTY (aside to LORD FANCOURT while he is playing). Here they are! Now don't forget the letter!

LORD FANCOURT. Oh, no, I won't forget.

KITTY (going to AMY up R.C.). Let's get them all out into the garden and leave her alone with Mr. Spettigue.

(*If the actor who plays* LORD FANCOURT *cannot play the piano, he can play "chopsticks" here.*

Enter SPETTIGUE, SIR FRANCIS, JACK *and* CHARLEY, *all in full evening dress, followed by* BRASSETT, *also evening dress; he stands by door with empty tray.* SPETTIGUE *comes* C., *stands as though entranced by music.* JACK *stands* L. *of* CHARLEY *down* R.C., *by ottoman.* SIR FRANCIS *joins* KITTY *and* AMY *up* R.C. BRASSETT *takes two empty cups from small table up* R.C.)

SPETTIGUE (*during last four bars of music—moves to* LORD FANCOURT, C.). Charming! Charming!

(LORD FANCOURT *stops playing; twirls round on stool and almost overbalances.* SPETTIGUE *saves him from falling. Then* LORD FANCOURT *sits staring at* ELA *on sofa* L.)

Bring the cigars, Brassett, unless the ladies— (*to* DONNA LUCIA) Mrs. Beverley-Smythe, (*to* LORD FANCOURT) Donna Lucia, do you object to—

LORD FANCOURT (*without thinking, using deep voice*). Smoking? Oh, no! I like it. (*Pulling himself up and using lighter voice.*) It kills the insects and things! (*Sits staring at* ELA *again.*)

(*Exit* BRASSETT, R.)

CHARLEY (*down* R.). Look at him, Jack.

JACK (R.C.). What's he doing?

CHARLEY. Staring at her like he did all through dinner.

JACK. The fool!

(BRASSETT *re-enters with cigars, cigar-cutters, matches on salver; he places them on table up* R.C. *and exits* R. *with salver.*)

SPETTIGUE (C., *aside*). I must make an opportunity to see her alone. *(Aloud.)* It's a sweet evening. Perhaps some of you may care to enjoy a cigar in the garden.

JACK. No, thank you, sir.

SPETTIGUE. It's a *sweet* evening. *(Goes up* C., *stands behind piano.)*

SIR FRANCIS *(with back to audience up* R.C., *facing girls).* You've been enjoying yourselves capitally, Miss Verdun, we heard the music.

KITTY *(to* SIR FRANCIS). Yes, Donna Lucia has been playing for us.

SPETTIGUE *(leaning over piano—to* LORD FAN-COURT). How charming of you, Donna Lucia! *(To* CHARLEY.) What should we have done without your dear aunt, Charley?

CHARLEY *(in hollow tone).* Oh!

JACK *(aside to* CHARLEY). Don't groan like that, you idiot! *(Going* C. *to* R. *of* LORD FANCOURT.) Are you fond of music, Mr. Spettigue?

(CHARLEY *joins* AMY *up* R.C.)

SPETTIGUE *(to* LORD FANCOURT, *with a look).* I—I hope to be.

(LORD FANCOURT *puts his hand on top of piano—* SPETTIGUE *covers it with his own.)*

LORD FANCOURT *(drawing hand away—slaps* SPET-TIGUE'S *hand with it).* Why—are you going to take lessons?

(SPETTIGUE *goes behind settee down* L., *and talks to* DONNA LUCIA *and* ELA.)

(Aside to JACK.) What's he looking at me like that for, like a boiled owl?

JACK *(taking* SIR FRANCIS'S L. *arm and bringing him down* C.). Dad, I'm glad you know about Kitty now, she's a splendid girl, isn't she?

(KITTY *crosses to* LORD FANCOURT.)

SIR FRANCIS. I like her very much, I must say, Jack.

JACK. You've taken a load off my mind, dad. I thought I was quite without means.

SIR FRANCIS. Not altogether, my boy. And you've thought this matter well over?

JACK. Night and day, dad, ever since I first met her.

(CHARLEY *goes down* R.)

SIR FRANCIS. It's a serious step, you know. *(Going down* R. *with* JACK.) A serious step.

(JACK *joins* CHARLEY *down* R.)

KITTY *(at piano, to* LORD FANCOURT). Now, don't forget—in writing. *(Goes to* AMY, *aside.)* Amy, let's get them all out into the garden. You take Charley. *(Goes down* R. *to* JACK.)

JACK *(aside,* R., *to* CHARLEY). I'm glad I told the dad now.

(SIR FRANCIS *joins* AMY *up* R., SPETTIGUE *joins* LORD FANCOURT *above piano.* KITTY *sits on ottoman,* JACK *stands* R. *of her.* CHARLEY *joins* AMY *up* R.C.)

SPETTIGUE *(leaning across piano, to* LORD FANCOURT). But why won't you listen to reason?

LORD FANCOURT. Of course, I'll listen to reason, but where is the letter?

SPETTIGUE *(recollecting, but without interest)*. Ah, I remember, I've not written it yet.

LORD FANCOURT. Not yet! *(Swings round on revolving stool to R., ending back to audience.)*

(SIR FRANCIS *goes to french windows* C., *and looks off.)*

SPETTIGUE *(spoonily)*. We must find an opportunity to talk it over, alone!

LORD FANCOURT. That will be nice! *(Swings back again L., turns, ending facing SPETTIGUE, each a three-quarter turn.)*

(SPETTIGUE *and* LORD FANCOURT *continue talking together.* SIR FRANCIS *crosses and stands behind piano up* L.)

AMY *(to* CHARLEY—*upstage* C.). But, Charley, why are you so depressing? We ought to be very happy today.

CHARLEY. Amy, great joys sometimes bring a—a sort of reaction; I shall be better— to-morrow! *(With a look at* LORD FANCOURT.)

AMY. Oh, come into the garden!

(Exeunt CHARLEY *and* AMY R.C. *window to* R. SPETTIGUE *crosses to table up* R.C. ELA *goes up behind piano to window* C. LORD FANCOURT *watching her— she turns and smiles to him—and exits immediately off* C. *to* L. SIR FRANCIS *drops down* L. *behind sofa to* DONNA LUCIA.)

JACK *(aside to* KITTY). I've told the dad blank out, and he's delighted! But, Kitty, you won't regret turning your back on "Society" and "The Row," and—?

KITTY. And the stifling hollowness of my own "Monday" and everybody's else's "rest-of-the-week" and

have something real to think about? Jack, the vista is
too heavenly. *(Rises.)* Come into the garden.

(JACK *and* KITTY *go up* C.)

SPETTIGUE *(up* R.C., *to* JACK). It's a sweet evening.
Perhaps you'd like a cigar, Jack. *(Offers cigar to
Jack.)*
JACK. No, thank you, sir.
SPETTIGUE. It's a sweet evening.

(Exeunt JACK *and* KITTY, C. *window to* R. SPETTIGUE
goes down R. LORD FANCOURT *starts to play again
softly.*
   NOTE.—LORD FANCOURT *to play here only if he
plays well. Nothing should be played to get a laugh
or to "guy"* SIR FRANCIS *and* DONNA LUCIA'S *exit.)*

SIR FRANCIS *(going* R. *of sofa).* Shall we join them?
DONNA LUCIA. Yes, it's a charity to leave those two
people alone.
SIR FRANCIS. Indeed, why?
DONNA LUCIA *(rising).* Only a little match-making
mischief, that's all. *(Going* C.)
SIR FRANCIS *(following* DONNA LUCIA—*between
her and* LORD FANCOURT *at piano).* On Spettigue's
account?
DONNA LUCIA *(Slyly).* No—on Donna Lucia's.

(DONNA LUCIA *and* SIR FRANCIS *exeunt window* C.
to L. SPETTIGUE *goes to window, watches them off.*
LORD FANCOURT *rises and hides behind piano.)*

SPETTIGUE *(joyfully).* They've gone! *(Turns, finds*
LORD FANCOURT *gone.)* Lucia! *(Coming down* C.)
They've gone!

(SPETTIGUE *looks about astonished, goes towards door*
R. LORD FANCOURT *strikes top note sharply on piano*

and retires quickly. SPETTIGUE *turns—*LORD FAN-
COURT *bobs up from behind piano.)*

LORD FANCOURT *(points playfully at* SPETTIGUE*).*
A-ah!

SPETTIGUE *(sees* LORD FANCOURT*).* Ah, there you
are! Lucia, how I have longed for this moment. *(Comes
to* C. *of piano.)*

LORD FANCOURT *(behind piano, "treble" end; aside).*
Oh, he's at it again. *(Goes upstage to "bass.")*

SPETTIGUE. Lucia, I must speak to you, I—

LORD FANCOURT. No. I am very angry with you.
(Puts hand on top of piano.)

SPETTIGUE Lucia, you wound me; don't say that!
(Moves to "bass.")

(Pats LORD FANCOURT's *hand.* LORD FANCOURT
snatches it away.)

LORD FANCOURT *(dodges to "treble").* But I do say
that—after the promise you made me, to treat me like
this. *(Unconsciously puts hand on piano top again.)*

SPETTIGUE. Promise?

LORD FANCOURT. The consent you promised in writing.

SPETTIGUE *(going to "treble").* Lucia, how can you,
when we have so much to say that more nearly con-
cerns ourselves. *(Pats* LORD FANCOURT's *hand lying
on piano.)*

*(*LORD FANCOURT *pulls hand away and smacks* SPET-
TIGUE's *hand.* SPETTIGUE *goes* R.C., *rubbing hand.)*

LORD FANCOURT. No, we have not. *(Coming* L.C.*)*
You don't know me! I'm no ordinary woman.

SPETTIGUE *(coming* C.*).* Lucia, I beg of you to listen
to me!

LORD FANCOURT. I'll listen to you with pleasure, but
where is the letter you promised me?

SPETTIGUE. Will you hear me, Lucia?

LORD FANCOURT *(getting rather annoyed and bored)*. I'll hear you with pleasure, *(going up* C. *to* R.*)* but why won't you give me the letter?

SPETTIGUE *(crossing* L.*)*. Lucia, do I deserve this?

LORD FANCOURT *(coming down* R.*; aside to* R.*)*. He deserves six months, the old idiot!

SPETTIGUE. Lucia, you are a puzzle, an enigma!

LORD FANCOURT *(crossing to* SPETTIGUE, L.C.*)*. How dare you! Until you give me the letter, all is over between us.

SPETTIGUE. Lucia, that decides me. I go to my room, *(casually)* a brief note—

LORD FANCOURT *(pointedly)*. With full consent and signed, don't forget.

SPETTIGUE *(at* L.I.E.*)*. Then say you will be mine?

LORD FANCOURT. I'll say anything you like, only don't be too long in the study.

SPETTIGUE *(at door* L.I.E., *kissing hand)*. Darling!

(Exits L.*)*

LORD FANCOURT (C.). That's all right! *(With surprise and amusement. Facing audience.)* I say, what devils we women are! *(Goes up to window* C.*)* It's too bad of those fellows! *(Going to piano, turns leaning against it.)* Why, I shall be an old woman for the rest of my life. I haven't had a drink or a smoke all day! *(Catches sight of cigar box on table* R., *crossing quickly.)* By George, here's a find! *(Looking towards door* L.*)* I wonder how long he'll be! Hanged if I don't chance it! *(Lights cigar with match which he strikes on his boot. Comes downstage* C., *puffs vigorously.)* Beautiful! Beautiful! *(Puffs.)*

(Enter DONNA LUCIA *with* ELA R. *of her, through* L.C. *window from* L.*)*

DONNA LUCIA *(sees* LORD FANCOURT *smoking—*

aside to ELA). She's smoking! *(Aloud.)* Ahem! *(Comes down L. side of him.)*

(ELA *comes down* R. *of* LORD FANCOURT. *He is startled, draws in a large mouthful of smoke, then hides cigar in placket hole, holding lighted end reversed in palm of* R. *hand—mouth full of smoke—looks from* DONNA LUCIA *to* ELA *and then straight ahead in agony, holding smoke first in opposite cheek to each one he looks at, then in both cheeks, screwing up eyes, almost bursting.)*

ELA *(this must be spoken through ensuing laughter or* LORD FANCOURT *would burst! Rapidly).* Auntie, did you find it chilly?

DONNA LUCIA. Yes, my dear, I thought I'd get a wrap of some kind.

ELA. I'll go upstairs and get you something. I know where your things are!

(Goes to door, turns, looks at LORD FANCOURT *and exits* R. LORD FANCOURT *looks after her. Blows out smoke and tries to wave it away.)*

DONNA LUCIA. Are you alone?

LORD FANCOURT *(comes* C.). Yes, I'm all alone—and so sad.

DONNA LUCIA. Dear me, *(sniffing smoke, crosses down* R.) what a dreadful smell of smoke! *(Secretly much amused.)*

LORD FANCOURT. Yes, I noticed it myself. *(Going quickly upstage, takes cigar out of placket hole and unseen, changes it into* L. *hand.)* I'll go and find out who it is.

DONNA LUCIA *(going up* R.C.). No, don't go.

(LORD FANCOURT *turns, holding cigar behind his back.)*

I wanted to talk to you.

LORD FANCOURT *(amiably)*. Yes. *(Comes down* L.C., *cigar behind back.)*

DONNA LUCIA. About your late husband, Dom Pedro.

LORD FANCOURT. Oh, that will be nice.

DONNA LUCIA. Do you know, when I met Dom Pedro, he told me he had no wife.

LORD FANCOURT. Oh, the wicked story-teller. Ah, but he was a cruel husband.

DONNA LUCIA. The Dom Pedro I knew was noble, kind and gentle.

LORD FANCOURT. That was his father, the old gentleman with the white moustache.

DONNA LUCIA *(aside, behind her fan, turning away)*. I never knew such effrontery! *(Returning* C. *Aloud.)* Do you know Donna Lucia, I'm surprised you don't indulge in the habit of smoking—so many Brazilian ladies do, you know.

LORD FANCOURT. Well, to tell you the truth, that's just what I was doing when you came in. *(Shows cigar in* L. *hand.)*

DONNA LUCIA. Then, pray don't let me interrupt you.

*(*LORD FANCOURT *smokes.)*

(Aside.) I shouldn't have been surprised at a pipe!

LORD FANCOURT *(stops smoking)*. Can I offer you one?

DONNA LUCIA. No thanks.

(Both turn, but LORD FANCOURT *kicks his skirt out of the way in turning—they go up* C. *together.* DONNA LUCIA *fans herself with* L. *hand—* LORD FANCOURT *does the same with* R. *hand.)*

You see, *(turning and taking his arm—both stop fanning—coming down* C.) not being a *Brazilian* lady, it might be thought strange. *(Letting go his arm.)*

LORD FANCOURT *(hopefully)*. Will you have a drink of any kind?

DONNA LUCIA. No thanks. Oh, Donna Lucia, pardon my curiosity, but—have you any children?

LORD FANCOURT *(taken off his guard, can't remember what he'd been told)*. Only a few—none to speak of.

(DONNA LUCIA goes up R.C. LORD FANCOURT goes down L. Re-enter ELA R. with wrap.)

ELA. Here's your wrap, auntie. *(Puts it on DONNA LUCIA's shoulders.)*

(LORD FANCOURT puts cigar in coffee cup on piano.)

DONNA LUCIA. Thank you, dear— I am going into the garden. I fancy Sir Francis has something to say to me. *(Going up C.)* And as it's rather chilly *(turning at window)* perhaps you'd better stay in!

(Exits C. to L. LORD FANCOURT steals a look at ELA about to exit, goes slowly to window L.C.)

ELA *(up C., coming down behind ottoman R.C.; quickly, aside)*. Auntie said we weren't to hint about our knowing she's not—auntie! I'm sure she's only doing it to oblige them.

(Turns, sees LORD FANCOURT about to exit window L.C.)

(Going up C. to LORD FANCOURT—aloud.) Oh, don't go—please.

LORD FANCOURT *(turns)*. I was going into the garden.

ELA *(R. of LORD FANCOURT)*. It has turned quite chilly. Auntie sent me in from the garden because of that.

LORD FANCOURT (*concerned*). Can I get you a wrap of any kind? (*Movement towards door* R.)

ELA (*stopping* LORD FANCOURT). No, thank you, auntie thinks I'm better here. I've been ill, you know.

LORD FANCOURT. Oh, but I didn't know.

ELA. Oh, I'm all right now, of course, if I take care.

LORD FANCOURT (*seriously*). Yes, you must take great care.

ELA (*taking* LORD FANCOURT'S R. *arm and going slowly down to ottoman* R.C.). Auntie, I fancy, is more particular than usual this evening—

(*Helping* LORD FANCOURT *to ottoman, puts cushion behind his back.*)

For, you know— (*quick look to* L.) years ago, she and Sir Francis (*kneels* L. *of* LORD FANCOURT) were— (*whispering*) sweethearts.

LORD FANCOURT. Were they?

ELA. But he went away—without telling her he was ever and ever so fond of her. Auntie says he was—shy, and he went away without knowing that she was ever and ever so fond of him. But the noblest man I ever knew was shy, and oh, so kind! (*With a look round.*) He got to know how papa had become so ill—and so poor—and lost a large sum of money to him at cards, auntie thinks, on purpose. I often wondered why they played cards, and papa so ill too, but when I asked the doctor if it wasn't doing harm, he said, "Not the game that was being played." (*A little pause.*) But I've got all the money and if ever we meet, I mean to give it back.

LORD FANCOURT (*quietly*). Oh, no, you must never think of doing that. It would be like accusing him of a sort of cheating, you know.

ELA. But it was so much—enough, auntie says, to make me independent for life.

LORD FANCOURT. And do you think he'd take it back if he knew that?

ELA *(simply)*. Oh, but I should feel it my duty—
LORD FANCOURT *(thankfully—smiling kindly)*. It's too late now.

ELA. But he went away before I had time to tell him how much I—I *(in a low voice)* loved him for *(rising)* —for his kindness to my poor father. *(Moves up* C.)

*(*LORD FANCOURT *rises quietly and goes round* R. *of ottoman up to* R.C.)*

(Turning. To LORD FANCOURT.) You don't mind my telling you all this, do you? I don't know why, but I like to talk to you. *(Putting her hand on his arm.)* I like you *(goes to window* L.C., *turning)* and I do so long to see him again.

(Exit L.C. *to* L. LORD FANCOURT *watches* ELA *off, then goes to ottoman down* R. *and punches cushion twice— vigorously. After cushion bus. Re-enter* SPETTIGUE *with letter,* L.)*

SPETTIGUE. Lucia!
LORD FANCOURT *(coming* C.). Have you got the letter?

*(*SPETTIGUE *shows letter.* LORD FANCOURT *tries to snatch it—* SPETTIGUE *holds it out of his reach.)*

SPETTIGUE. Yes, here is the letter. But first, make my happiness complete. Say that from this blissful moment we are engaged?
LORD FANCOURT. We are engaged.

*(*LORD FANCOURT *gets the letter.)*

Got it—we are engaged. *(Going to door* R.)
SPETTIGUE. Darling!
LORD FANCOURT *(turning)*. Mr. Spettigue!

SPETTIGUE. Call me Stephen.

LORD FANCOURT (*reading letter*). Is this the letter—Stephen?

SPETTIGUE. Yes, that is the letter and we are betrothed?

LORD FANCOURT (*at door* R.). We are betrothed, darling!

(*Quick exit. Enter* SIR FRANCIS *and* DONNA LUCIA, C., *window from* L.)

SPETTIGUE (*going up to* C. *opening, shaking* SIR FRANCIS *by both hands*). Ah, Mrs. Beverley-Smythe, Sir Francis, congratulate me, congratulate me! (*Going up to* R.C. *window.*)

(SIR FRANCIS *looks puzzled.*)

DONNA LUCIA (*coming down* R.—*aside*). I knew it.

SPETTIGUE (*in* C. *window, turning*). I'm the happiest man in the world—but where are the dear children? This must be a day of happiness and rejoicing for us all, for us all!

(*Exits* C. *to* R.)

SIR FRANCIS (*coming down* C.; *taking* DONNA LUCIA's *wrap off and placing it on back of ottoman*). What on earth does he mean? What's all this excitement about?

DONNA LUCIA (*sits on ottoman,* R.C.). Can't you guess?

SIR FRANCIS. No.

DONNA LUCIA. Didn't I tell you what would happen if we left them alone?

SIR FRANCIS. Eh?

DONNA LUCIA. Don't you understand? She's accepted him.

SIR FRANCIS. What?

DONNA LUCIA *(drily)*. Yes, Donna Lucia d'Alvadorez! *(Sits on ottoman.)*

SIR FRANCIS. You don't mean that?

DONNA LUCIA. I fancy he'll find out his mistake before long.

SIR FRANCIS *(half aside)*. By George, what a fool I've been!

DONNA LUCIA. Why? Are you sorry?

SIR FRANCIS (R.C.). No, but—that rascal of a boy of mine made some sort of a stupid suggestion that I should—

DONNA LUCIA. That you should offer your hand and heart to Donna Lucia d'Alvadorez—from Brazil, where the nuts come from.

SIR FRANCIS. When I think of what a fool I was— might have been—should have been—

DONNA LUCIA. Then you don't envy him?

SIR FRANCIS. Envy him! *(Coming to her* R.)

DONNA LUCIA. But think of her millions.

SIR FRANCIS. Ah, Lucy, when I saw your face—

DONNA LUCIA. You didn't recognise it!

SIR FRANCIS. No, but when I did—but I told you all that in the garden just now—and you'll be content for a while with a cottage and your old sweetheart?

DONNA LUCIA. And you? You would take me, a penniless widow?

SIR FRANCIS. Nothing could make me happier!

DONNA LUCIA *(gives him her hand)*. Frank!

SIR FRANCIS *(taking her hand)*. Lucy!

(A little pause. DONNA LUCIA smiles.)

Why, what are you smiling at?

DONNA LUCIA. I was only thinking of—

SIR FRANCIS. Of what?

DONNA LUCIA. Of Donna Lucia d'Alvadorez.

(Enter ELA L.C. window from L.)

SIR FRANCIS. Well, she's a quaint little figure, I must own! *(Goes up* R.C. *to* R. *window.)*

ELA *(coming down to* DONNA LUCIA, R.). Auntie, did you find the air chilly?

DONNA LUCIA. I didn't notice, my love.

ELA *(laughing)*. Auntie, how pretty you look to-night! *(With look to* SIR FRANCIS, *whispering.)* Has Sir Francis—?

DONNA LUCIA. Ssh!

*(*ELA *kisses* DONNA LUCIA *and sits on ottoman,* L. *of her.* SIR FRANCIS *comes down* R. *and sits on chair below door* R.)

SPETTIGUE *(off)*. Come along, my dear children— *(entering)* —come along!

(Enter SPETTIGUE, R.C. *window, followed by* KITTY *and* AMY, JACK *and* CHARLEY. BRASSETT *enters door* R., *carrying salver, goes up* R.C. CHARLEY *up* C., JACK L. *of him.)*

(Coming down to front of sofa, L.C.) Kitty, you sit there, *(indicating piano stool)* Amy there. *(Stands* R.C. *by* ELA.) I have something to tell you. Something you will all be very pleased to hear. *(Looking round.)* But where is Donna Lucia?

(General movement. No one answers—then BRASSETT *steps forward.)*

BRASSETT *(in front of small table up* R.C.). Donna Lucia's gone to her room, I fancy! *(Steps back again.)*

SPETTIGUE. Ah, perhaps it's just as well! Now, before she returns, I have a little secret to tell you.

(All exchange glances.)

ALL. A secret? Oh, really? *(etc.)*

SPETTIGUE *(cutting in, rather louder, to gain attention).* I am sure you will pardon me if I ask your attention for a few moments.

CHARLEY *(aside to* JACK, *quick and low).* Good gracious, Jack, what's he going to say?

JACK *(aside to* CHARLEY, *quickly).* How do I know till he's said it?

SPETTIGUE. Situated as I am, a lonely widower, a mateless uncle—surrounded with grave responsibilities —my ward— *(indicating* KITTY), my niece— *(indicating* AMY), a good fairy has, I may say, tripped in among us, bringing with her unexpected light and joy!

CHARLEY *(aside rapidly to* JACK). Who does he mean?

JACK *(aside rapidly to* CHARLEY). Shut up!

SPETTIGUE. Under her influence, I have consented to the engagement of my niece to a gentleman in whose honour and probity I have the fullest confidence—Mr. Charles Wykeham.

(CHARLEY *goes to* AMY R.C., *and takes her hand.*)

AMY. Charley, how sweet of your dear aunt.

SPETTIGUE. Furthermore, charmed by irresistible spells, I have consented to the union of my ward with John, only son of my friend, Sir Francis Chesney.

(JACK *goes to* KITTY.)

(Pointing to carnation in his coat.) Ah! Sir Francis—

(SIR FRANCIS *laughs.*)

But what will you say to a *third* engagement?

(CHARLEY *returns* C. *to* JACK.)

OMNES. *(they look at him breathlessly).* {A third? {What?

SPETTIGUE. Our good fairy—nay, let me add without further metaphor *(rather pompously)* —one whose name is honoured in the South-Western hemisphere as that of Rothschild is in Europe *(self-consciously and rather smug)* —has consented to become Mrs. Stephen Spettigue.

(KITTY *rises.*)

I allude to our dear friend, Donna Lucia d'Alvadorez.

(BRASSETT, R.C., *holding empty tray behind his back, knocks it against table and it falls with a loud clatter on to the floor. General movement of surprise— everyone starts. CHARLEY joins JACK up L.C., leaving BRASSETT in full view.*)

SPETTIGUE *(furious)*. What is that?
BRASSETT *(looking helplessly R. and L. and nervously shooting first one cuff and then the other)*. Beg pardon, sir—the tray, sir.

(KITTY *pushes music stool under piano, and goes to back of sofa.*)

SPETTIGUE *(shouting)*. Be more careful, Brassett—

(BRASSETT *picks up tray.*)

AMY *(coming forward—conciliatingly)*. Uncle!
SPETTIGUE *(more quietly)*. Be more careful. *(Resuming speech.)* Nothing could please me more than—
CHARLEY *(breaking forward, wildly—coming down C. to SPETTIGUE)*. Mr. Spettigue, I can listen to this ghastly farrago no longer.
SPETTIGUE. Mr. Wykeham, sir—what do you mean?
CHARLEY. I say, sir—and I don't care what the result may be—I can listen to this ghastly—

SPETTIGUE *(loftily—breaking in)*. I presume, sir, in espousing my niece—

CHARLEY *(wildly—cutting in)*. I can't— I won't espouse her— *(Consternation and general excitement. AMY turns away, goes up R.)* —under these false and lying pretences!

(DONNA LUCIA *smiles.*)

That woman—

SPETTIGUE. Do you allude in such a manner to—

CHARLEY. I say that woman—

SPETTIGUE. I must beg of you to speak with more respect of your aunt.

CHARLEY. She is *not* my aunt!

(DONNA LUCIA *rises—followed by* ELA, *and goes up* C., *watching the following scene from there.* SIR FRANCIS *goes round back of ottoman to top end of piano.* BRASSETT *goes to door* R.)

SPETTIGUE. Not your aunt! What do you mean?

CHARLEY. I love Amy far too sincerely to—

SPETTIGUE *(excitedly)*. Never mind that, sir; explain your words!

JACK *(coming forward)*. Mr. Spettigue—will you allow me to say that the blame is mine—and let me explain?

SPETTIGUE. I am addressing this person. *(To* CHARLEY.*)* Answer me, sir, explain your words.

BRASSETT *(at door; aside)*. I must tell his lordship of this!

(Exit R.*)*

CHARLEY. At the last moment, this morning, my aunt —on whose account we had invited Miss Verdun and Miss Spettigue—telegraphed to say she couldn't come. The ladies arrived and we—

JACK *(helping* CHARLEY *out).* And I, sir, prevailed upon another person, to—well—

SPETTIGUE. To personate her. *(Crossing* R. *below ottoman.)* I've been treacherously, infamously deceived!

CHARLEY *(crossing* R.C. *to* SPETTIGUE*).* That was not our intention, sir!

SPETTIGUE *(turning, furious).* Don't lie to me, sir.

*(*CHARLEY *goes up* R.C. *to* R. *of* AMY, *who turns away from him. He stands above door* R.*)*

JACK *(trying to calm* SPETTIGUE*).* I beg your pardon, sir, you forget you were not expected.

SPETTIGUE *(below door* R.*).* A frump like that, with a wig!

JACK. Well, you can't blame her for that. *(Joins* KITTY *behind sofa down* L.*)*

LORD FANCOURT *(off).* May I come in?

(Anxious looks from JACK *and* CHARLEY *to door* R.*)*

SPETTIGUE *(savagely).* Turn that woman out of my house!

(Enter LORD FANCOURT *in man's evening dress* R. *General movement of surprise.* KITTY *goes to end of sofa.)*

LORD FANCOURT *(coming* C.*).* I say, may I come in?

SPETTIGUE. Turn that woman out of— *(Turning, sees* LORD FANCOURT—*breathlessly.)* Who are you, sir?

LORD FANCOURT *(*R.C., *holding hands in front of him like an old lady).* I'm Charley's aunt from Brazil where the nuts come from.

*(*KITTY *goes to front of sofa.)*

JACK *(going* C.; *aside to* LORD FANCOURT*).* Fancourt Babberley!—you duffer— *(Goes above sofa L. to* Kitty.)

Lord Fancourt *(to* Spettigue*)*. Fancourt Babberley, I beg your pardon.

Ela *(aside to* Donna Lucia*)*. Auntie! And I told him everything!

(They go out c. *window for a minute.)*

Spettigue *(still furious)*. What does this mean, sir?

*(*Donna Lucia *returns* c., Ela *by top end of piano.)*

Lord Fancourt *(to* Spettigue*)*. It means that we've all done very wrong and we're all extremely sorry, and tender you our humblest apologies—my apologies, I should say, for if I hadn't offered the temptation, the whole thing would never have occurred.

*(*Ela *moves quietly down* L.C. *to front of piano stool.)*

Charley. And if Mr. Spettigue will allow us to add our apologies—

Jack. And say we have no words to express our contrition—

Spettigue *(raging)*. It's infamous, infamous! But where is the document obtained from me under these fraudulent pretences?

Lord Fancourt. Oh, the letter, I have the letter! *(Produces it from inside breast pocket of dress coat.)*

Kitty *(below sofa)*. It's mine, mine!

Spettigue *(to* Lord Fancourt*)*. Give it to me. *(Seeing* Kitty's *anxiety.)* Miss Verdun! *(To* Lord Fancourt.*)* Sir. I demand it! *(Coming forward to take it.)*

*(*Lord Fancourt *holds up letter in* L. *hand.)*

Donna Lucia *(down* c.*—interposing)*. Allow me. *(Takes letter.)*

SPETTIGUE. I shall dispute it—under her father's will. I shall dispute it.

DONNA LUCIA. This letter is addressed, and has been delivered to Donna Lucia d'Alvadorez.

SPETTIGUE But she— *(catching* LORD FANCOURT's *eye)* —I mean he—is not Donna Lucia d'Alvadorez.

DONNA LUCIA. No—but I am!

SPETTIGUE. You!!!⎫
ALL. You!　　　⎬ *(together).*
SIR FRANCIS. Lucy!⎭

(General movement of surprise and exclamation. KITTY *sits on sofa.* DONNA LUCIA *joins* SIR FRANCIS *up* L.C. *by piano.)*

CHARLEY *(tiny pause—quick gasp).* My aunt! *(Said unconsciously, like the slang expression.)*

SPETTIGUE. You will pardon me if I retire. *(Goes below ottoman to door,* R. *Turning to* LORD FANCOURT.) As for you, sir, I shall enquire from the authorities, your college—in the morning.

(Opens doors, about to exit, stops, takes out button-hole and throws it C. *Exits* R. LORD FANCOURT *catches carnation and goes to door* R.)

LORD FANCOURT *(turning, grabs* CHARLEY's *right arm).* Charley, can he have me up for breach of promise?

AMY *(up* C., *coming forward—indignantly to* CHARLEY). Charley, *(stamping foot)* Mr. Wykeham, I mean—how dare you? I'll never forgive you! I'll never forgive *any* of you, for treating uncle Stephen like that! *(Turns to exit through window.)*

DONNA LUCIA *(*C., *stopping* AMY, *taking her hand).* Be patient with us, my dear. Your uncle shall have the most profound reparation my influence can make. For my own part *(to* SIR FRANCIS) I only shared in the deception when I found *(to* LORD FANCOURT) another lady established in my place.

LORD FANCOURT *(to* CHARLEY). No wonder she knew all about my late husband.

(DONNA LUCIA *hands* AMY *over to* CHARLEY. *All talk together.)*

KITTY. Well, I'm as sorry as anyone, but I'd trust Jack with my life.
DONNA LUCIA *(coming down to* L.C.). Indeed? Then he must wait till I'm his mother.

(CHARLEY *and* AMY *go down* R. AMY *sits on ottoman.* CHARLEY *stands* L. *of her.)*

JACK *(turning to* DONNA LUCIA). Mother?
SIR FRANCIS *(coming down* C. *to* R. *of* DONNA LUCIA). Yes, Donna Lucia, in deceiving me as much as anybody, has, however done me the honour to recollect an old affection, and has promised to assume that authority—so look out, Jack!

(SIR FRANCIS *retires above piano.* JACK *sits on sofa* R. *of* KITTY. ELA *moves down to top end of piano.)*

DONNA LUCIA (C., *to* LORD FANCOURT). Lord Fancourt Babberley—

(LORD FANCOURT *comes* C. *to* R. *of* DONNA LUCIA.)

I am afraid you have gained one confidence that nothing could excuse.
LORD FANCOURT. I know, and I reproach myself beyond expression *(looking at* ELA), but I wouldn't part with the memory of that confidence to save my life, and if Miss Delahay will allow me to say so, I am willing to atone for it, with a life-long devotion.

(DONNA LUCIA *looks at* ELA, *then holds out* L. *hand to her.* ELA *smiling, puts hers in* DONNA LUCIA'S.)

ELA. Auntie!

(DONNA LUCIA *hands her across to* LORD FANCOURT. LORD FANCOURT *takes* ELA's *hand and tucks it in his arm and as they turn to go up* C. LORD FANCOURT *kicks the front of* CHARLEY's *leg with his instep as he passes.* CHARLEY *limps round behind ottoman to* R. *of* AMY.)

DONNA LUCIA (*turning to* JACK). Now, where's my son?
JACK (*rising*). Here, "mamma"!
DONNA LUCIA. I shall have to talk to you very seriously before I give you *this.* (*Shows letter.*)

(JACK *sits again.*)

(*Turning to* CHARLEY, C.) Charley, I'll never forgive you if you deceive that sweet girl again! (*To* LORD FANCOURT.) And as for you, sir—

(*Orchestra starts to play curtain music very softly as in Acts I and II.*)

LORD FANCOURT (*coming down* C., *with* ELA *on his* R.). Oh no, never again, I give you my word. I'll give you the clothes if you like, I've done with them. Miss Delahay has consented to think me over as a husband, and in future I resign to Sir Francis Chesney—

(SIR FRANCIS *has come down between* DONNA LUCIA *and piano during last speech.*)

—all claims to "Charley's Aunt."

(*Music swells to forte.*)

CURTAIN.

CHARLEY'S AUNT

FURNITURE AND PROPERTY PLOT

Act I

Carpet on floor, Parquet stage-cloth and 6 dining-room oak chairs, 1 saddleback armchair with white antimacassar, revolving office chair, flat-topped pedestal writing table 4-ft. 6 in. oak dining-room table, sideboard, with cupboard under, upright piano (or open bookcase, 6-ft., filled with books). Long red rep fabric window curtains. Hanging wall mirror. Letter-basket, blotter, 2 pens, with leads instead of nibs, inkstand, separate single sheet note-paper, envelopes size larger. Corona cigar box. A.B.C. Time Table (remove half the pages and fasten together with string to make it lighter for throwing). Waste-paper basket. "Strand" magazine. Books, Photos. Pile of music (or books, if no piano). Picture post cards of actresses (1892 period) on mantelshelf. Vase, four cushions, 2 magazines, "Sketch" and "Tatler," stationery rack. Brass tray. Decanter, with whiskey, jug of water, 3 glasses, 4 champagne (wooden) property bottles, 1 claret bottle (real).

Old plaster bust of Plato and pedestal. Old mortarboard, cap and gown.

1 white sweater, 1 white muffler, 1 pair of oars lettered St. O.C.B.C. and dated 1891 and 1892. Photo "rowing eight group."

Off stage down L.

Clock.

Knocker.

Boxing gloves and single sticks.

For CHARLEY.

Cheap watch and leather strap.

Copy of "Truth" open at paragraph and marked with red pencil, then folded in half to go in pocket.

Telegram and envelope.

For BRASSETT.

Letter addressed to C. Wykeham Esq., St. Olde's College, on blue notepaper.

Small parcel of hairpins tied with string and a loop to carry it by.

Very large dress box tied with string.

Butler's tray laid with tablecloth, 5 table-napkins, 5 plates, 5 knives and forks, 5 dessert-spoons, 1 serving-spoon and fork. Entree dish and lid with lobster salad. 5 rolls, 5 champagne glasses, 1 claret glass. Tablecloth folded over everything and sides of tray turned up.

For SIR FRANCIS.

Bills (one extra long) fastened together, also cheque made out and signed. Carnation button hole, deep cerise red, which will show up well against LORD FANCOURT's white lace fichu, and yet not be too bright on SIR FRANCIS' suit.

For AMY.

Bouquet of flowers, either roses or carnations and maidenhair fern (mounted on short stick which is bound with green ribbon) and wrapped in white tissue paper.

Off stage, up L.

Table, wig block, mirror, chair and lights for LORD FANCOURT's quick change.

Off stage, up R.

For LORD FANCOURT:

Old Gladstone bag.

For JACK:
    Pipe.
Noise effects. Knocks with knocker off L.

ACT II

Description of Scene.

Lawn with walls on either side, and at the back a corner of the College with stone walls, and the windows and door to Jack Chesney's rooms as plan. The back-cloth would show other parts of the grounds with other colleges in the distance.

PROPERTIES

Knocker on door to Jack Chesney's rooms and under-neath is painted "Mr. John Chesney."
1 small round wicker or white wrought iron table.
1 rather large ditto square table.
1 wicker or white wrought iron rustic chair.
2 wicker or white wrought iron or rustic armchairs with 5 "river" cushions in one R.C.
Stage-cloth grass and flagged pavement.

Props off on table behind door up C. *in housepiece.*

For BRASSETT.
    Cigarettes, matches, ashtray on brass salver.
    Afternoon teacloth.
    Large silver tea-tray with 5 cups and saucers and teaspoons.
    Sugar-basin, milk-jug *full* of milk, teapot *full* of strong *boiling* hot tea filled just before end of act.
For SIR FRANCIS.
    Popgun (or cicycle-pump with attached cork on end of string) to make the sound of a cork being drawn.

Props off, down L.I.E.

For SPETTIGUE.
Top-hat with tin lining for his last entrance.

Props off, up R.

For DONNA LUCIA.
Several visting-cards—one engraved "Mrs. Beverley-Smythe."

Noise effects.—The pop of a cork being drawn up C. in Jack's rooms.

ACT III

Victorian sofa with cushions.
1 clover-shaped ottoman with centre pillar (Victorian "redan").
Single drawing-room chair down R. below doors.
Single chair between each of the sets of french windows.
1 small writing bureau.
2 china cabinets.
1 stool at writing bureau.
1 upright Victorian piano.
1 revolving music stool.
1 carpet (or 3 rugs, one in front of sofa, one in front of double doors, one in front of C. french windows).
Several pictures.
Ornaments (various).
China for cabinets.
1 tall white china vase of red and pink peonies.
1 brass bowl with syringa.
3 cushions.
1 floor standard lamp (imitation Victorian oil) and Victorian shade.

1 lamp (imitation Victorian oil) with Victorian shade, on bureau.

Chandelier centre gas (or gas brackets on walls).

1 small occasional table with ash-tray and matches.

Victorian window curtains and velvet over-mantel.

Typical Victorian curtain over door L. looped up in Victorian manner.

Props off, by door R.

Down R. Table, mirror, chair and light for LORD FANCOURT'S quick change.

For ELA.

Green bottle of smelling salts.

For DONNA LUCIA.

Large and beautiful feather fan.

Evening wrap.

For BRASSETT.

Long narrow silver tray with 5 coffee cups, saucers and spoons, and sugar and cream-jug (cups painted inside to look as though they were filled with coffee).

Round salver with cigar-box and cigars (one cut and pierced with a hat-pin to make it draw easily).

Round salver to drop.

For LORD FANCOURT.

Letter for SPETTIGUE in R. inside breast-pocket.

For SPETTIGUE.

Wears carnation.

Off, up L.—Letter in envelope.

CHARLEY'S AUNT

LIGHTING PLOT

GENERAL SETTING

Floats and No. 1 Batten.—2 circuits white, 1 circuit pink, 1 circuit light amber.

No. 2 Batten.—2 circuits white, 1 circuit light amber.

No. 3 Batten.—1 circuit white, 1 circuit light amber, 1 circuit mixed.

No. 4 Batten.—1 circuit white, 1 circuit light amber, 1 circuit blue.

Stage Floods.—4.

Stage Spots.—1 (1,000-watts).

Lengths.—2 long white and amber, 2 short white and amber.

Front of House Spots (if any).—2

Perches (if any).—2 O.P., 2P.

ACT I

Floats.—1 circuit white (FULL), 1 circuit white (half), 1 circuit light amber (FULL).

No. 1.—2 circuits white (FULL), 1 circuit light amber (FULL).

No. 3 (or 4).—1 circuit white (FULL), 1 circuit light amber (FULL), 1 circuit mixed white and amber.

Lengths.—L.1 E. amber and white length (4 white, 4 amber).

L.U.E. amber and white length (4 white, 4 amber).

Stage Floods.—1 left of C. window or backcloth (straw).

1 right of C. window or backcloth (straw).

1 1,000-watt spot L. of C. window shining through on to seat.

Perches.—Top O.P. on desk R.

Bottom O.P. on chair L. of desk.

Top P. on chair R. of table.

Bottom P. on chair downstage C.

Front of House Spots (if any).—1 straw on desk R.C. (open FULL), 1 straw on table C. (open FULL).

ACT II

Floats.—1 circuit white (FULL), 1 circuit white (half), 1 circuit light amber.

Battens 1, 2, 3 and 4.—2 circuits white (FULL), 1 circuit amber (FULL).

Lengths.—L.U.E., 1 small white and amber.

Window L., 1 small white and amber.

Stage Floods.—L.I.E., 1 straw.

Arch R.C., 2 white.

R.I E., 1 straw.

Perches.—Top O.P. on chair behind table C.

Bottom O.P. on chair L. of table

Top P. on chair behind table C.

Bottom P. on chair R. of table.

Front of House Spots (if any).—1 straw on arch R.C. (open FULL), 1 straw on table C. (open FULL).

ACT III

Floats.—1 circuit straw, 1 circuit pink.

No. 1 Batten.—1 circuit straw, 1 circuit pink, 1 circuit white (half).

No. 4 Batten.—1 circuit blue (18).

Lengths.—L.U.E. amber and white (4 and 4).

R.U.E. amber and white (4 and 4).

Stage Floods.—1 L. of window C. on to window (No. 17).

1 R. of window C. on back-cloth (No. 18).

Perches.—Top O.P. on piano stool L.C.
  Bottom O.P. on sofa L.
  Top P. on stage C.
  Bottom P. on clover leaf seat R.

Front of House Spots (if any).—1 light pink on sofa L.
  (FULL open), 1 light pink on clover-leaf seat R.C.
  (FULL open).

Fittings.—1 imitation Victorian standard oil lamp.
  1 imitaton Victorian oil table lamp.
  Chandelier C. (imitation gas) or wall brackets (imitation gas).

CHARLEY'S AUNT

DESCRIPTION OF DRESS, PETTICOAT, WIG, BONNET, FICHU AND FAN.

Light brown wig, centre parting, straight hair drawn flat against face to top of ears, then tightly plaited. These plaits go under ears and join with the small plaited knob at the back of the neck. The wig must grip firmly. The wig is worn as far back on the forehead as possible, and on the top is sewn the bonnet, showing about 3 inches of hair in front.

Cap.—Black Chantilly or Spanish lace, mounted on net cap to fit above the bun of hair with small elastic grip to go under bun of back hair, lace wired rather high in front with 2 small bright red roses slightly to L.C. Black lace streamer at the back, which is secured to the black net. This should be about 6 inches longer than the net cap. This again is trimmed down the centre with a cerise ribbon pleated to an inch wide with 3 small flat cerise bows sewn across it at regular intervals. Each side of the face hang two black corded ribbon streamers 2½ inches wide and 15 inches long and are put on with a pleat just under folds of lace level with the ears.

Black silk mittens, black satin fan on narrow black satin ribbon to hang from wrist.

White lace fichu shaped at the back of the neck so as to lie flat on the back, falling with a deep point just above waistband at the back and well below waist in front—this takes 3 yards of lace, 15 inches wide. It should half-cover the sleeves at the side.

White lace collars and cuffs 3 inches deep—the lace should be slightly turned in at the neck to make it narrower for the collar.

Large cameo pinchbeck brooch fastens the fichu together high up at neck on the collar, and the fichu is looped over once at waist.

Petticoat.—Stiff cotton moire, made with deep 11-inch frill at the foot, pleated at waist into band and fastened with placket at right front. Large black bone button and buttonhole in waistband.

Braces.—Two pieces of elastic 1¼ inches wide for braces, sewn on to petticoat waistband at back, crossed and stitched together in middle of back. In the front they have a buttonhole cut and worked in the elastic, and a button each side on the petticoat waistband. The length of the petticoat should be just to show the hem of LORD FANCOURT's trousers.

Dress.—Very stiff black satin, the same as the facings that dress-clothes are made of. Otherwise cotton-backed satin. Very full skirt gathered into 3-inch waistband with a short placket-hole at the right front. A little more fullness on hips than centre back, and slightly less eased across front and large black bone button and buttonhole in waistband. The deep 5-inch hem is interlined with buckram, and the whole dress lined with black sateen, and the skirt has a rouleau of black velvet inside the foot of the hem, to save wear on hem, but this must not show. The skirt should just touch the ground evenly all round.

Bodice.—Flat pleated bodice, set into 3-inch waistband, and stiff plain satin upright collar high and loose enough just to cover LORD FANCOURT's own collar and tie. This fastens centre with two very large hooks and steel eyes, or patent clips. The flat lace collar should not be quite as deep as the collar on dress. The bodice fastens down centre front with six large black bone buttons and buttonholes, the last to be in centre of waistband. The skirt is continued on this waistband and fastened on the right front with another large button and buttonhole in waistband. The sleeves are large, full, bell-shaped, finishing in stiffened satin cuffs 4 inches deep, and extra wide to go on very easily. The top of the sleeves are stiffened with interlining of tailor's canvas. The bodice and skirt are joined together into the waistband.

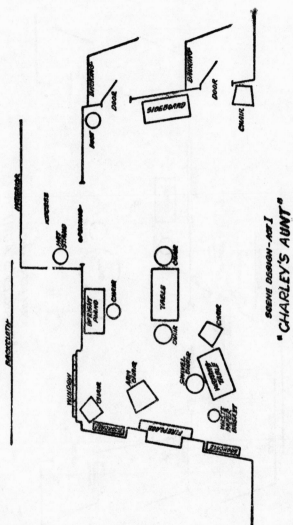

SCENE DESIGN—ACT I
"CHARLEY'S AUNT"

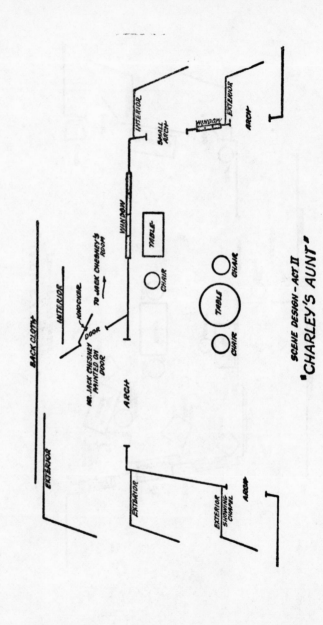

SCENE DESIGN – ACT II
"CHARLEY'S AUNT"

SCENE DESIGN – ACT III
"CHARLEY'S AUNT"

BACKCLOTH

FIREPLACE

BACKING

DOOR

CHINA CABINET

FRENCH WINDOWS

SOFA

UPRIGHT PIANO

CHAIR

STOOL

FRENCH WINDOWS

CHAIR

CLOVER-LEAF OTTOMAN SEAT

FRENCH WINDOWS

CHINA CABINET

CHAIR

BUREAU

DOUBLE DOORS

BACKING

CHAIR